Prep

Prep

The Parent's Guide to Boarding Schools

Kristin White

BLOOMSBURY ACADEMIC
NEW YORK · LONDON · OXFORD · NEW DELHI · SYDNEY

BLOOMSBURY ACADEMIC
Bloomsbury Publishing Inc, 1385 Broadway, New York, NY 10018, USA
Bloomsbury Publishing Plc, 50 Bedford Square, London, WC1B 3DP, UK
Bloomsbury Publishing Ireland, 29 Earlsfort Terrace, Dublin 2, D02 AY28, Ireland

BLOOMSBURY, BLOOMSBURY ACADEMIC and the Diana logo are trademarks of Bloomsbury Publishing Plc

First published in the United States of America 2025

Copyright © 2025 by Kristin White

All rights reserved. No part of this publication may be: i) reproduced or transmitted in any form, electronic or mechanical, including photocopying, recording or by means of any information storage or retrieval system without prior permission in writing from the publishers; or ii) used or reproduced in any way for the training, development or operation of artificial intelligence (AI) technologies, including generative AI technologies. The rights holders expressly reserve this publication from the text and data mining exception as per Article 4(3) of the Digital Single Market Directive (EU) 2019/790.

Bloomsbury Publishing Inc does not have any control over, or responsibility for, any third-party websites referred to or in this book. All internet addresses given in this book were correct at the time of going to press. The author and publisher regret any inconvenience caused if addresses have changed or sites have ceased to exist, but can accept no responsibility for any such changes.

Library of Congress Control Number: 2025932455

ISBN: PB: 978-1-53819-799-8
ePDF: 979-8-76515-477-9
eBook: 978-1-53819-800-1

Typeset by Deanta Global Publishing Services, Chennai, India
Printed and bound in the United States of America

For product safety related questions contact productsafety@bloomsbury.com.

To find out more about our authors and books visit www.bloomsbury.com and sign up for our newsletters.

Contents

Introduction	vii
I: Evaluating and Applying to Boarding Schools	**1**
1 Boarding School 101	3
2 Will Boarding School Help My Child Get into a Better College?	17
3 Campus Visits and Interview Preparation	31
4 Applications and Testing	43
5 Financial Aid and Scholarships	55
6 Inside the Admissions Committee	67
7 Is Boarding School the Right Choice?	81
II: The World of Boarding Schools	**91**
8 Life at Boarding Schools	93
9 Athletics at Boarding Schools	107

10	The Arts at Boarding Schools	129
11	International Students at Boarding Schools	137
12	Students with Learning Disabilities or ADHD at Boarding Schools	147
13	Postgraduates at Boarding Schools	159

III: Types of Boarding Schools		**167**
14	Ultraselective Boarding Schools	169
15	Single-Sex Boarding Schools	175
16	Junior Boarding Schools	179
17	Military Schools	185
18	Unique Boarding Schools	189

Appendix: Directory of Boarding Schools by State	199
Notes	211
Bibliography	217
Index	221
About the Author	233

Introduction

People often ask me how I came to be a boarding school expert, especially since I didn't attend boarding school myself. It all started in college, where I developed an interest in education and helping kids find life-changing paths for themselves. I was a volunteer tutor and the director of the Georgetown University Sursum Corda Literacy Program, where I had the joy of reading with elementary school kids every week.

My fellow tutors and I, concerned about the quality of the public schools our students were attending, were able to arrange scholarships for a few of the children to attend a Catholic elementary school in the Georgetown neighborhood of DC. When our first four students came to our tutoring session in their school uniforms, excitedly telling us about their bus ride across the city and all the new kids and friendly teachers they had met at their school, we felt victorious, wondering if perhaps there was even more we could do. Our group of tutors graduated from Georgetown, started a nonprofit, and raised money both to continue funding Catholic school scholarships and to look for more opportunities. We knew that many of the children of Sursum Corda had difficult situations at home, with parents who were struggling either financially or with addictions, health, or emotional issues. We saw the immediate benefits of providing our students with a scholarship to a school across town, and it led us to wonder, What strides could our students make and what doors would be opened if they attended boarding schools?

The first student I advised for a boarding school placement was a boy named Jeremy, who lived with his elderly grandmother in a public housing development in DC. With test scores that were off-the-charts high, as well as an insatiable curiosity and love of science, he seemed like a young man who was ready to take a step forward in his education and in his life. Jeremy's grandmother agreed to consider boarding schools as long as they were close to home. I spoke with the admissions team at Episcopal High School, which is just outside of DC, and they helped Jeremy—and me—through the application process. They welcomed Jeremy into their freshman class, and they kindly counseled me on the ins and outs of boarding school admission. Jeremy's success at Episcopal was only the first step. In the next few years, I helped Inika find her way to Linden Hall, Eric to Blair, and Earl to New Hampton.

I found great satisfaction in helping teenagers find life-changing educational opportunities that shaped their futures in a positive way. I started a career as an independent educational consultant and began the work of helping families discover the world of boarding schools. Over the years, I have visited almost one hundred boarding school campuses, and I have had the privilege of working closely with parents as they navigate their child's future education plans. It's been almost twenty years since I helped Jeremy find his way to Episcopal, and in that time, I have worked with many hundreds of boarding school applicants from across the country and the world.

In my work with families, I realized there were many misconceptions and misunderstandings about boarding school.

Some families came to me after getting rejected at all the schools they applied to, and others first spoke to me after enrolling at a school that was not a good fit for their student. I realized that although there is a lot of information about boarding schools online, there is no resource that offers analysis and insight into boarding school admissions. *Prep: The Parent's Guide to Boarding Schools* will be the first boarding school book in print in many years, and I hope it offers insight, guidance, and encouragement to families who are embarking on the boarding school application process.

I hope that parents will use this resource to learn more about boarding school life and culture, and I hope it will help them to choose a list of schools for their child that are academic, social, and financial fits. My goal is to provide a resource that will guide parents through the process, from start to finish, and help them feel confident about their choices without needing a consultant or placement professional.

This book includes examples of real students and parents with whom I have worked. Their names have been changed to protect their privacy, and in some cases, an identifiable trait or school name was replaced with a similar one. I hope that you will find their stories encouraging and insightful as you learn about the exciting world of boarding schools.

I

EVALUATING AND APPLYING TO BOARDING SCHOOLS

1

Boarding School 101

It's easy to be drawn into the mystique and glamour of boarding schools. You may be intrigued by what you see in movies, television shows, or books, or you may associate boarding schools with successful people and great opportunities. No longer seen as exclusively for the wealthy, boarding schools offer opportunities for students from all backgrounds. Parents know that these schools can offer a transformative experience, one that can positively impact a young life. But where do you begin in determining which schools to consider, when to apply, and how to go about this process? The first step is to evaluate your family goals for high school and how a boarding school could help your child on his educational journey.

IS BOARDING SCHOOL RIGHT FOR YOUR CHILD?

Parents consider boarding school for many different reasons. One family may be in search of academic support, while another is looking for greater academic rigor, and yet another family may simply be looking to make a school change for social reasons. Ultimately, it's about opportunity and helping your child achieve in their academics, social endeavors, and extracurricular pursuits. The following are common reasons that parents consider boarding schools for their children.

Community and Friendship

Boarding schools are vibrant, 24/7 communities full of opportunities for interactions with peers and faculty members. Your child will build relationships with a variety of students, which will be well beyond the typical high school friend group. Whether they are baking brownies in the houseparent's apartment with friends from their dorm, working in the library at night with their study group, or participating in a Saturday field trip, kids at boarding school are busy, engaged, and involved with their peers. Parents with children who spend too much time on screens are drawn to the active boarding school lifestyle, where there is not only less time for social media and gaming but often less interest in it due to all the personal interactions and activities available.

Personal Growth

Boarding school students learn to be independent. They do their own laundry, coordinate their weekend schedule, and manage their own sleeping, working, and socializing routine. They have the help of supportive adults but often make profound gains in independence and self-confidence. Academically, boarding school students are encouraged to self-advocate by asking for help and building relationships with their teachers. They experience personal growth by getting to know students from other states and countries, which gives them a broad worldview. They have the opportunity to try new extracurricular activities, and in many cases, the boarding school schedule gives them the time to pursue several areas of interest at once. For parents who think that their child has the potential to do more, grow more, and have positive experiences outside of the home, boarding school may be the answer.

Academic Support

Many boarding schools offer a community of academic support, which includes nurturing teachers who are available for one-on-one meetings, as well as individual learning plans. Students with learning disabilities or ADHD benefit from the structured learning support programs at boarding schools. Some students, whether they do or do not have learning disabilities, may benefit simply from being in an environment where teachers are available, classes are small, and students generally make positive academic strides forward.

Academic Rigor

Many students go above and beyond in their classes and are eager for greater challenges. They may be in honors courses but still seek extra work through online classes, summer programs, or local accelerated math courses. These students want a high school experience that involves more projects, discussions, and deeper dives into academic subjects. Many boarding schools offer an advanced level of academic work, whether it is math beyond the calculus level, pre-engineering classes, or courses with extensive writing and discussion, in which students can find rigorous course material, higher level discussions, and enthusiasm for learning.

Opportunities in Sports or the Arts

Young athletes today are often highly specialized, playing their sport year-round on travel and club teams. Some are drawn to boarding school for a chance to play on a top-ranked team, while others may want to try a sport not offered in their area, such as squash, rowing, or field hockey. Or they may come from a school that cuts students from the sports teams, and by attending boarding school, they will have the chance to make the team. Likewise, for activities in the arts, such as band, orchestra, or theater, students can get the chance to participate and excel in these areas. Best of all, the boarding school schedule often allows for students to be involved with both sports and the arts.

English Language Learning

For students whose first language is not English, immersion is crucial for achieving fluency. Parents overseas know that it is essential to learn and practice English at a young age. Some boarding schools offer English language learner programs which help students who are not yet fluent in English. For those who are comfortable speaking English, the immersive environment of an American boarding school can help students achieve fluency and even graduate sounding like a native speaker.

Improvement of Home Situation

Some families are faced with local schools that are not strong or do not meet their student's needs. Sometimes, the peer group is not motivated; other times, the student has had difficulties with friendships and wants to start fresh socially. There may be conflict within the home, and a boarding program may offer needed structure and consistency. For any of these reasons, boarding school offers an opportunity to start anew in a supportive environment.

Student Readiness

Sometimes, it is the student who is driving the decision. Many teenagers see boarding school as an adventure, a chance to be part of a social and fun community, or as an opportunity to excel in their area of interest. They may have become aware of boarding schools through friends, club sports teams, social media, TV, books, and/or movies. Many parents are led to the world of boarding schools by their enthusiastic children.

Parents should consider their child's readiness for boarding school before embarking on the admissions journey. If your student has been successful and happy at sleepaway camp, that is a good sign that he will enjoy the structured days and camaraderie of boarding school life. If she hasn't been to an overnight program, does she feel ready to try, or does she show independence in other ways? Boarding school isn't for everyone, and it's important to consider if your child would thrive in this environment.

THE PARENT PERSPECTIVE

Many parents today don't miss a game or performance and are happily involved in their teen's daily life. How can they agree to let their child leave home for boarding school? In truth, it is a small adjustment for some parents—and a painful sacrifice for others. I've seen parents approach the prospect of boarding school in several ways. First, there are parents who are unbothered by the separation, since they know they will stay connected through texts, phone calls, and frequent visits and vacations. Then there are families who will only consider boarding schools within a few hours' drive so that they can continue to attend school events and visit frequently. There are a small number of parents who rent or buy a home near their child's boarding school. This second home allows them to be present in their teen's life while also providing a relaxing space for their teen. It is an expensive proposition, but it has grown more popular with the increase in the number of people working remotely. The final type of boarding school parent is the one who makes a great sacrifice, feeling the separation with their child but knowing it is for the best.

Xin, my client from Shanghai, China, dropped off his fourteen-year-old son, Zack, at a boarding school in Massachusetts. "He is our only child, our world. Everything we do is for him. His life would be harder if he stayed in China. We think the best thing for Zack is to go to high school and college in the United States," Xin explained.

Xin's wife, Ling, told me, "When we finally left him on move-in day, everything was good. Zack and his roommate were about to leave for a dorm pizza party, and we smiled and encouraged him, hugged him, and then we left. When we started to drive to the airport, my husband broke down and was crying so much that he had to pull over into a CVS parking lot. We cried there for a long time. What people passing by must have thought of us! It's hard to leave your child halfway around the world in a new place. Most people will never understand what that's like."

For Xin and Ling, boarding school represented both an opportunity and a sacrifice. It was difficult to leave their son, but once Zack was there, he thrived, and the experience turned out to be everything they had hoped it would be. They chose a school that had an advisory program, houseparents who connected frequently with parents, and a school culture that welcomed parental involvement. They joined a Chinese parents' text group and a parents' committee, and they communicated with their son daily and with his advisor weekly. They felt welcomed and included in the school community, and they never regretted their decision to send Zack to boarding school.

IN WHAT GRADE SHOULD MY STUDENT START BOARDING SCHOOL?

Ninth grade is the most common entry point for boarding school, which aligns with the start of high school. This is the grade level that brings the greatest number of applicants, but it also has the most spaces available. Students starting in ninth grade benefit from entering with a large cohort of new students, and they participate in the full four-year program, with a chance to grow into school leadership roles.

In tenth grade a boarding school class gets bigger, as additional new students are joining. For some, fifteen years old is the right age to try boarding. With one year of high school completed, they come in with maturity and experience. Public school students sometimes find that the large high school experience wasn't for them, and they are ready for a boarding community for the remainder of their high school years.

Eleventh grade is another common entry point, with most boarding schools enrolling several new students, and some enrolling as many as twenty or thirty. New juniors are sixteen or seventeen years old, ready for independence, and eager to face the challenges of improving their transcript and extracurricular profile for college admissions.

It's rare—but not impossible—for a new student to join in the twelfth grade. Phillips Exeter is one of the few selective boarding schools that welcomes applications from new seniors.

Many boarding schools enroll "postgraduate," or "PG year," students. These are young adults who have graduated from high school but choose to embark on a fifth-year experience. Originally, the PG year was designed for young men who wanted to play a sport in college or needed more time to physically and emotionally grow for college. Today, the PG year is used by both boys and girls who attend a fifth year at prep school for academic, social, or athletic reasons.

A small number of students begin the boarding experience in middle school. These eleven- to fourteen-year-olds often start at "junior boarding schools," which are focused on fifth- to ninth-grade boarders, providing a warm environment with a specialized focus on tweens and young teens. Because junior boarding schools end in eighth or ninth grade, these students must apply to a new school for their high school years. Many of the single-sex schools and military schools offer boarding programs that span both middle and high school, and a few coed schools—for example, Perkiomen, Wilbraham and Monson, and Ethel Walker—offer boarding for both middle school and high school students

REPEATING, OR "RECLASSING"

In the boarding school world, a phenomenon called "reclassing" occurs when a student repeats a year while changing schools. It had been called repeating a grade in the past, but since students aren't repeating any classes, the more accurate term is *reclass*. For example, a student may be in ninth grade at their local school and then apply to boarding school to enter as a ninth grader. A family may decide to reclass so that their student can have more time to mature and personally grow, to improve in his sport (which may help with recruiting), to improve grades, or simply to have more time, taking five rather than four years of high school coursework to present to colleges. Reclassing is more common with boys than girls, since they mature later academically, socially, and physically. It's important to note that students who reclass do not repeat courses. If a student finished Spanish 2 and geometry in ninth grade, for example, he would move on to Spanish 3 and algebra 2 in his second ninth-grade year.

At some boarding schools, as many as a third of the incoming ninth-grade boys have already completed ninth grade at their home school. Other boarding schools report that about 15 percent of their incoming students have reclassed. Eleventh grade is another common reclass year, and some schools report that 75 percent of their new eleventh-grade boys are repeating the grade.

The decision to reclass is left to the family, and applicants will see a question on the application that asks what grade the student is applying for. Parents should consider the pros and cons of reclassing. Yes, the student gets the gift of another year, a chance to improve and grow, but the financial cost of an additional year is high. And while most students have only benefited from reclassing, other students find it difficult to be in high school at nineteen years old, when their peers are in college.

WHEN TO START RESEARCHING AND APPLYING?

I recommend that families start investigating boarding schools a year to a year and a half before the intended enrollment date. This leaves them time to get to know the schools and put their best feet forward in the admissions process. The first step is to research and develop a list of schools of interest. The application period opens in the fall of the year prior. For example, a student applying for ninth grade will be busy with the application process in the fall of her eighth-grade year, completing everything by January 15 or February 1, two common deadlines. These schools will notify applicants of their decision to admit, deny, or wait-list on March 10. The families are invited to "revisit days," and then they have until May 1 to decide which school to attend.

But of course, there are some families who are late to the game and only decide to consider boarding school in the winter, spring, or even summer of that school year, well after the deadline. However, there are many schools that are eager to get late applications from these students. If a school still has room, they will continue to review applications until they are fully enrolled. The very selective and well-known schools are typically fully enrolled on the May 1 decision date, but others have space available into the summer. Some schools even have availability for midyear or immediate enrollment. The best way to find out about late admissions, immediate, or midyear enrollment is to call admissions at each school of interest and ask if they are still considering new applicants.

HOW TO RESEARCH AND LEARN ABOUT SCHOOLS

I hope that this book will be your primary source for learning about the schools and the boarding school admissions process. It's also important to research online, meet with school representatives, and visit campuses. After all, boarding schools are all about the people, and it's important to get to know students and staff and to get a sense of the school culture to see if it is a fit for your student. These resources will help you to do that.

School Websites

The best source of information is the school's own website. It includes information on curriculum, signature programs, student life, college advising, and the admissions process, among many other topics. I encourage parents to look at the School Profile, which is a document that every high school sends to colleges with their students' applications. It may include the courses offered, AP test scores, SAT scores, GPA distribution, number of National Merit Scholars, and demographic information. I use the School Profiles to compare schools and to get a sense of the academic rigor and achievements of the student body. School websites have a collection of videos that include campus tours, student interviews, or panels on specific subject areas or programs. Students can find contact information and photos and biographies of staff members on the websites. It can be helpful to look at the bios of the admissions staff when preparing for your interview or, after your interview, to look back for contact information before sending your thank-you emails.

Social Media

We get so much information from social media these days, and the boarding school world is no exception. Not only does each school have its own Instagram account, but often, the school admissions office has its own account with postings geared toward applicants, and many sports teams or student groups have their own Instagram updates. This is a great way to get insight into the school community from different perspectives.

Websites and Internet Research

When I work with students, I often send them YouTube videos about the specific boarding schools on their lists.

They love the short videos, some of which are made by students and others produced by the school. If you go to YouTube and search by a boarding school name, you will find a variety of official and unofficial videos related to the school.

The Association of Boarding Schools website (www.boardingschools.com) is an excellent resource about boarding school life and includes a search function to identify schools of interest.

Boarding School Review (www.boardingschoolreview.com) is a website that is aesthetically dated but has links to videos and information on schools across the country that can be helpful in your research.

Niche (www.niche.com) has a function to search by state for boarding schools and offers more updated reviews and data on both day and boarding schools.

Boarding School Fairs

Whether you live in Bangkok, Seoul, New York, Dallas, or many other places around the world, you can meet admissions representatives, get some swag, and learn more about educational options at a boarding school fair. These events are free, casual ways to talk one-on-one with school representatives and to learn about their offerings. The Parents League of New York has operated a fair annually since 1975, which is now one of the largest in-person fairs. The Parents League, as well as other groups, including the Ten Schools Admission Organization (https://www.tenschools.org), also offers virtual fairs, which include panel discussions and comments from students and faculty. To find a boarding school fair, look at the admissions websites of schools of interest, as they usually post their travel schedule. Students who complete the inquiry forms on a school's admissions page will receive emailed invitations to fairs in their area.

Educational Consultants and High School Placement Advisors

Many families, facing questions or uncertainty about the boarding school admissions process, turn to professionals for help and guidance. Educational consultants, high school placement advisors, and counselors from education access programs are three types of professionals who support students in identifying schools and helping them through the admissions process. I have worked in all three roles, as I got my start in this field at a nonprofit in Washington, DC, that supported students from underrepresented groups in boarding schools and colleges. I then went on to work as an educational consultant and as the director of high school counseling at a K–8 independent school in Connecticut.

Students who attend K–8 or K–9 private schools get help from their school's high school placement advisor, who is a staff member, much like a college counselor at a high school helps with college placement. Participants in education access programs, such as A Better Chance or Prep for Prep, work with counselors who help them navigate the admissions process. If you don't have a school or program counselor to help you, you could consider hiring an educational consultant. My firm, Brightbridge Advisors (www.brightbridgeadvisors.com), works with students from all over the world. You can find other educational consultants through IECA, the Independent Educational Consultants Association (www.iecaonline.com), whose members are the best in the industry. Member consultants are required to have experience and connections in the field, and they must abide by ethical standards.

Campus Visits

It's the people at the schools who make up the boarding school experience, and an in-person visit is the best way to meet teachers, students, and staff, as well as to observe campus life. Some boarding schools offer open house visits in the fall, while others only welcome visitors who sign up for an interview and campus tour. Chapter 3 includes more details about the interview and visit, which is an evaluative part of the admissions process.

BUILDING A SCHOOL LIST

It's important to consider your family preferences when building a list of schools. One family's must-have might not even rank as a valued characteristic for another family. I suggest starting with distance from home and location. Families who live within driving distance of boarding schools may prefer options within a three-hour drive so they can participate in their child's school life. Parents who live overseas may prefer a school that is fairly close to an airport for ease of commuting and visiting, or they may prefer a school with a high percentage of boarders so that their child will have a full and busy campus on weekends.

Admissions selectivity is crucial to consider, and it is the one area where parents often go wrong. I have met with families who call me after the application process and report that their child was denied or wait-listed at all the schools they applied to. They feel disheartened and regretful of all the time and money spent visiting and applying to schools, plus the effect it has on their child, who was turned down everywhere. Selective schools deny many applicants who are fully qualified, so it is important to make a list that includes schools with a range of selectivity.

For some families, the public school or their local private school is their "safety" or backup option, but for others, they need to consider schools that are likely to accept their child. One way to get an opinion on a school list that is a right match in admissions selectivity is to work with an educational consultant who has experience in boarding schools. If you are going through the process on your own, you can gauge a school's selectivity by looking at the acceptance rate, the average SSAT score, and the School Profile from the college counseling office, and you can ask school representatives about their typical accepted-student profile. Once you have a list of schools to apply to, you are ready to move on to the application phase of the admissions process.

**CHARACTERISTICS TO CONSIDER
WHEN BUILDING A SCHOOL LIST**

Distance from home or proximity to an airport
Suburban or rural campus
Large or small student population
Coed vs. single sex
Percent of boarders vs. day students
Diversity of students and faculty
Academic program and rigor
Learning support services
Activities offered
Religious or nonsectarian
Admissions selectivity

2

✣

Will Boarding School Help My Child Get into a Better College?

The idea that boarding schools have a stronghold on elite college admissions is held as a fact by some parents, and it drives them to enroll their children at these schools. You may have heard or read statements like the following:

> "Boarding school guidance counselors have a special connection to college admission deans. They talk and are able to get kids in."
> "Colleges know that kids at top private schools are well prepared. They can get Bs and still get into top colleges since they want these kids so badly."
> "Exeter and Andover are feeder schools to the Ivy League."
> "It's like horse trading—our college counselor will tell students, 'You can't apply to Duke, since there is someone else I will place there, but I can get you into Dartmouth. I will talk to them and make sure it all works out.'"

And as parents, that's what we want—for it all to work out. Parents know that selective colleges are harder to get into than ever, and they have heard about students with top grades who were denied at colleges that were once considered fairly easy to get into. They are concerned about the competitive economic landscape their children will be facing when they start their careers. Parents want their children to be successfully launched—to have a secure and fulfilling job, home ownership, and a prosperous future.

To many, the most assured path to that life is through a selective college. They feel this will lead to better job prospects, as well as strong personal and career connections with other successful people. Parents are hopeful that attending boarding school will help their child be a more compelling college applicant, whether that is through improved qualifications or simply getting a special boost for graduating from a well-known school.

This view that boarding schools offer a smoother path to college admissions success is often supported by the schools themselves. The list of colleges that have accepted their seniors has long been used as a marketing tool by private schools. It's common in my area of Connecticut to see the local private schools take out a half-page ad in the newspaper announcing the college matriculation of their graduating class. These results are also featured prominently on each school's website. At open houses and informational meetings, the head of school will often discuss the college placement process and results with prospective families. It's easy to come away from this with the idea that attending private school—specifically, a boarding school—will give your student an edge in the college game.

But will it? Let's look at the evidence and viewpoints.

WAYS THAT BOARDING SCHOOL WILL HELP WITH COLLEGE ADMISSIONS

The positive personal growth that students at boarding schools experience often results in a stronger profile and better results in college admissions. This isn't to say that these students are seeing better results solely due to the reputation of the school but that these teenagers have become better students and candidates for college because of how they thrived and grew at boarding school—and how this is presented to colleges. Let's explore how that happens.

Teacher and Counselor Recommendations

Boarding schools pride themselves on producing excellent teacher and counselor recommendations for college. At many schools, they are peer-reviewed, with each teacher sharing their letter for suggestions and approval before submitting. This ensures that they take the time, include relevant details and anecdotes, and give an overall favorable review. Teachers at boarding schools know the students not only through their classes but also from extracurricular activities and dorm life, making it easier for them to write about nonacademic attributes. A recent study on admissions at highly selective colleges shows that one important way wealthy students and private school students have an advantage in admissions is through higher nonacademic ratings,[1] and teacher recommendations are an important way to showcase these attributes.

At public schools, teachers typically have a large batch of recommendation letters to complete, and they may not have the chance to get to know their students well. Letters are often formulated from questionnaires the teachers give to their students. Some high schools have student-to-counselor ratios that are as high as five hundred to one, and thus, their school counselors will often decline to write college recommendation letters for their students. Colleges understand that counselors are overworked and can't effectively write several hundred letters in an admissions season. They do accept students from these schools, but the lack of a guidance recommendation is a missed opportunity for the colleges to hear about a student's nonacademic interests and leadership.

An admissions officer at a selective college said to me, "The private school teacher recommendations are usually glowing. They cover more and go into more depth. Sometimes, they are really selling the student to us, though, and there are teachers who give high reviews to everyone, so we do realize that they are not impartial."

In addition to the written narrative, a Common Application teacher recommendation form includes a grid where teachers are asked to rate the student in attributes such as intellectual promise, quality of writing, creative thought, leadership, productive discussion, and more. Teachers are asked to rate the student as: average, below average, excellent (top 10 percent), outstanding (top 5 percent), or as one of the top few encountered in a career.[2] These ratings are important but can serve to dissolve some of the boarding school advantage. When rating students, especially when there are several from the class applying to the same colleges, there is less they can do to help "sell" the student, since colleges will closely compare students by school.

Improving Grades

Many boarding school students see an immediate bump upward in their grades and are able to maintain this level throughout high school. Since grades are known to be the most important factor in college admissions, this is one clear way that boarding schools can help a student in the college admissions process. But how does this happen?

Boarding schools offer an intensive learning environment. Students attend study hours in the evenings, which require a break from social media and other distractions. Teachers are on duty during this time, checking to see that students are working, offering review sessions before a test, or meeting with students to go over concepts or to revise an essay. These extra hours of academics are helpful to all students but especially to those who have trouble getting homework done, preparing for tests, or focusing and concentrating. The study hours with teacher support are a key reason that some boarding school students see a positive increase in their grades.

Many boarding schools also offer a learning center that gives support and instruction to students with learning differences or ADHD. Staffed with a team of learning specialists, these trained professionals work with students on executive functioning skills and learning strategies. They often coordinate with the student's teachers and work with students either one-on-one or in small groups. For students who have struggled academically, these learning support programs can be life changing. My clients who attended boarding schools with learning support saw not only an improvement in grades but a gain in self-confidence and an ability to picture themselves being successful in college.

A third factor that leads to an improvement in grades for boarding school students is the structured environment that is enriched by peer groups. Admissions committees will often handpick a group of students who are academically focused and interested in being part of a community. They are students who are joiners, who want to get involved, and who want to improve their skills in sports, the arts, or whatever their area of interest may be.

Even though teens today are drawn toward gaming and social media, at boarding school, there is simply less time for it, and with so much face-to-face interaction with peers, students aren't looking to electronics to connect as often as other teens are. Kids at boarding school often buy in to the campus culture, and that includes doing their best academically. That feeling of being motivated, wanting to do well, and spending less time on screens can be contagious.

Luke was a sophomore who had mostly B grades and an occasional C while at his Pennsylvania public high school. He had been cut from the soccer team and spent a lot of time gaming after school. Luke enrolled at Trinity Pawling as a junior, and his grades rose to the A range, with just one B, in the first semester. When I asked him how this had happened, he said, "It's mainly the study hours. I never spent so much time studying before, but this is what everyone is doing. And the teachers are around to help." I also noted that Luke was able to make the soccer team at Trinity Pawling (most boarding schools have room on their sports teams for any student who wants to participate), and being back on a team, along with a busy schedule and peer group, made Luke happier and helped him to focus and earn the grades he wanted for college admissions.

But it's important to note that not all students will see an improvement in their grades, because many boarding school applicants already have straight As. Certainly, successful applicants to elite boarding schools have shown that they are successful in their school's curriculum and have gone above and beyond, perhaps taking summer school courses or showing an academic interest outside of school. I was at a boarding school admissions meeting with multiple school admissions deans from selective schools who were discussing the idea of grade inflation, or how difficult it is to evaluate applications when so many students have all As. One school admissions dean said of the middle school and high school students applying to his school, "It's rare to see a B on a transcript these days."

If your student has not yet reached his potential academically, a boarding school may offer the structured environment, learning support, and positive peer group and school culture that will help him improve his grades and be a better candidate for college. But if your student is already strong, with mainly As, and is likely to continue to be a strong student no matter where she goes to high school, then it's not likely that her college admissions prospects will get a boost from the grade improvement often seen at boarding schools.

Extracurricular Activity Opportunities

College admissions committees look for students with deep involvement and passions, those who help others and are involved in their school communities. On the college application, students are asked to list and describe their activities, and in some cases, there are supplemental essays asking for more details about this involvement. Since college deans are looking to shape a class of students who will contribute to campus life, they greatly value the student's extracurricular involvement.

Activities and involvement are areas where boarding schools truly shine. They offer more than a typical high school and allow students the time they need to take on multiple activities. It's common for a student to be a member of a sports team, sing in the school musical, and be involved in clubs. Students are not likely to get cut from a sports team, shut out of the play, or denied a spot on the debate team when they attend boarding school.

It is often difficult to make the sports teams at many public and private day schools. There may be one hundred boys trying out for a soccer team that will only take fifty total on its varsity and junior varsity (JV) teams, or there are sixty girls trying out for JV and varsity tennis teams that can carry only twenty-four on their roster. It can be devastating for a teen to be cut from a sport she loves, and it can also leave a void on her college application. At boarding schools, this is not likely to happen. They have a smaller student population to start with, so it's unlikely that they would have so many students trying out for one sport. They typically offer varsity, junior varsity, and "thirds" teams, which are for students who don't make the top teams. Most boarding schools are committed to allowing all students to play their preferred sport, and some have added varsity B teams, or thirds B, teams.

Boarding school students are able to find leadership roles, start their own clubs and groups, and be a part of robotics, debate, Model UN, or other groups without a competitive application process. For students who haven't found their extracurricular area of interest, it is not too late for them to explore new programs and clubs and find a way to get deeply involved.

One of my clients found that attending boarding school and trying a new activity was instrumental in his acceptance to college. Carson was from Arizona and attended a large public high school where he played basketball and got good grades, but he was often bored and unchallenged. He and his parents wanted a more motivated peer group for him, as well as a school with more advanced classes and opportunities. He enrolled at Kent, where, as a sophomore, he tried rowing for the first time. He ended up excelling in this sport, which led to competitions overseas, national recognition, and interest from many college coaches. Carson committed to the rowing program at Princeton University and was admitted in the early decision admissions round. He went on to enjoy his life as a scholar-athlete at Princeton, a college he would probably have not been admitted to without rowing.

Riley felt lost in her large public school. She hadn't made any connections with clubs or activities, and she was cut from the field hockey and tennis teams during her sophomore year. She applied to boarding school and attended Pomfret for her junior and senior year. Not only was she able to play the sports she loved, but she was named captain of the field hockey team. She got involved with a volunteer program, Model UN, and her class council. She was able to show involvement, leadership, and commitment on her college application and was happily admitted to Middlebury College.

English Language and Culture

For international students, attending boarding school in the United States can help them in the college admissions process. The students can improve their English language skills through immersion, and they can become familiar with American culture and academics. They have the opportunity to take the SAT or ACT on campus and to benefit from the school's college counseling support. International students are able to present a transcript in English, which comprises a curriculum that the colleges know and understand. Additionally, they benefit from the reputation of their boarding school, as the colleges know their school, have had students apply and enroll, and can trust and understand the grades and teacher recommendations. International students are able to participate in sports, the arts, and all the activities available at a boarding school, many of which are not offered overseas.

I worked with a student from China named Ruby, who attended a public school in Shanghai. She worked on her English with a tutor but didn't have the opportunity to take classes in English, and she didn't feel that her English conversation skills were getting any better. Ruby's parents had a goal for her to attend college in the United States, so they planned for her to come to America for a full-immersion high school experience. She enrolled in Miss Hall's School as a ninth grader and quickly became fluent in English and involved in school life. Ruby was accepted at many colleges and enrolled in Babson College to study entrepreneurship.

DOES PRESTIGE ALONE HELP IN COLLEGE ADMISSIONS?

"Are Bs at Choate, Exeter, or the equivalent equal to As at other schools?" I have been asked a variation of this question many times over the years. And I can unequivocally answer, "No." A student with all Bs at an elite boarding school is not a strong candidate for selective colleges. Some parents think their bright child will get "bonus points" for going to a selective independent school, hoping that the name alone will open doors. And while there certainly are benefits to attending boarding school, and the student who emerges after a boarding school education may indeed be a better college candidate, I have not seen a boost in college admissions on name alone.

As an educational consultant who works with both boarding school and college admissions, I have a client list for college admissions that includes a mix of students who attend elite boarding schools, independent day schools, and public schools. Recently, I worked with three girls who had very similar profiles but attended different types of high schools.

One girl attended an elite boarding school; the other, a top-ranked public school in Fairfield County, Connecticut; and the third, a respected independent day school in Westchester County, New York.

The girls' profiles were strikingly similar. They had unweighted GPAs in the 3.8 range, meaning they had mostly As with a few Bs. They all had the same ACT score of 32, and each had taken two AP exams during junior year, scoring a mix of 4s and 5s. They had typical, active school involvement in sports, volunteer work, and leadership. Each of the girls talked with me about their dream colleges, which included Duke, Georgetown, and Princeton, but they realized that their grades, testing, course rigor, and activities were low for these colleges. My client at the elite boarding school was not given better odds, and in fact, her school counselor encouraged her to be realistic, to look at admissions statistics, and to apply to a broad range of colleges.

When the acceptances arrived and final decisions were made, the girl from the elite boarding school decided to attend Wake Forest University. And as it turned out, the girl from the Fairfield County public high school also enrolled at Wake Forest. Their academic profiles led them to similar colleges, despite the fact that one attended an elite boarding school and one was a graduate of a public school. This is just one example, but it illustrates the point: it is the student who is being evaluated, not the high school.

Counselor Calls

When my father was a senior at a Jesuit prep school in 1957, his admission to Georgetown University was arranged through his head of school and the college admissions office. He doesn't remember sending an application or taking an SAT, only receiving word from the headmaster that he had spoken to someone at Georgetown and they would be welcoming him to their freshman class. In those days, there were fewer applicants, and it was common for colleges to form connections with high schools that would ensure the flow of new students with good credentials into their universities.

That type of strong connection dimmed over time and, eventually, became what is called the "counselor call." It was no longer a deal being made but simply a discussion between a well-connected private school's college counselor and a college admissions dean. The counselor had the chance to advocate for their students, put in a good word, and perhaps even put some pressure on the dean to accept the students being discussed. But while this counselor call may have been prevalent twenty years ago, it is rare now. With the tremendous increase in applications, college admissions deans don't have the time to talk with college counselors. And frankly, they often don't have the interest in doing so, as they feel that their application process provides all the information they need to make a decision.

Jim Jump, college counselor at an independent school and former president of the National Association for College Admissions Counseling, writes in *Inside Higher Ed*,

> Early in my career, it was common to have a call with admissions officers at institutions where my school regularly sent applicants before decisions were finalized. It was a discussion, not a negotiation, but I had the ability to ask for a second look at candidates on the bubble. Occasionally a decision would be changed from deny to waitlist or waitlist to accept. Gradually the nature of counselor calls changed to a reporting function, providing context on the applicant pool that helped us explain decisions to students and parents. At some institutions those calls more resembled infomercials, with the message often sounding like "We're so excited that we could reject so many of your students."[3]

Jump then quotes a *New York Times* article on diversity in independent schools: "A letter or call from the counselor at a top private school can work wonders with college admissions offices." It is an example of a false statement that adds to the mystique around independent schools and college admissions. Jump asked colleagues in school counseling to respond to the article, and many reacted with "a mix of sadness and hostility." They did not see their role as a lobbyist or as one who impacted admissions decisions, and they felt that the idea harmed their profession, their work, and parental expectations.

Jim Jump then wrote, "It's time to retire the college-counselor-as-Hollywood-agent trope," that it is time to end the urban legend that school counselors are making deals and having influence in the admissions process at selective colleges.

And in fact, many of the colleges already have. Christoph Guttentag, dean of admissions at Duke University, announced on an informational Zoom call that Duke would no longer accept counselor calls. Other colleges have followed suit, citing the lack of time in conducting these calls, the ethical question of allowing it, and the fact that these calls were not helpful to college admissions deans, since their applications provided all the information the committee needed to make a decision.

WEALTH EFFECT AND CORRELATION WITH COLLEGE ADMISSIONS

A recent study showed that students from the top 1 percent of income levels in the United States are more than twice as likely to attend an *Ivy Plus* college as those from middle class families with the same scores.[4] The term Ivy Plus refers to colleges that are in the Ivy League or are equally competitive, such as MIT, Duke, Johns Hopkins, Georgetown, or others. It's not surprising to see that wealth is correlated with elite college admissions, since tuition is expensive, as is test prep, and so are the costs of activities, tutors, and other things associated with the life of a high achieving high school student. Since we know that boarding schools have many students from high-income families, it's important to consider that the impressive boarding school college matriculation list could be correlated to the wealth of the students who attend rather than to the school itself.

The study shows three factors that drive the high-income advantage: legacy admissions, recruitment of athletes, and higher nonacademic credentials. The first category is for children of alumni who apply to their parents' colleges and are accepted at a greater rate. This accounts for 46 percent of the wealth preference in admissions. The study shows that recruited athletes, as the majority come from high-income families, represent 24 percent of the wealth preference. But it is the third category, the nonacademic credentials, with 30 percent of the wealth preference attributed to it, where boarding schools have the most potential to make a difference. What this category says is that colleges assign higher ratings for nonacademic credentials, which includes leadership roles and extracurricular activities, to wealthier students and private school students. This makes sense since we know that boarding schools offer more opportunities for activities and give more detailed and thoughtful teacher recommendations.

The results of the study ring true with what I have witnessed in the admissions environment. When working with wealthy students, I see many with legacy connections or those with backgrounds in extensive sports training programs that smooth their pathway to elite colleges. The third category says that wealthy students and those in private schools have better nonacademic credentials. I see this with boarding school students, who have the opportunity to get involved in more sports, arts, and other activities; to earn leadership roles; and even to start new clubs. They have more time in their schedules and encouragement to pursue these activities. And just as important, the teacher and guidance recommendations include a thoughtful and thorough narrative about these nonacademic activities and traits.

The decision to attend boarding school is a personal one for each family. College admissions success should not be the primary driver for the decision to attend boarding school, but I realize that it is one of many factors that parents consider.

Rather than looking at boarding school as a boost in admissions for all students, it's important to look at it in the context of your own family situation.

If your student needs learning support, finding him a school with a strong learning center can be life changing. If he needs to improve his grades, a boarding school with a focused study hall, lots of teacher help, and a motivated peer group will be helpful to improving his candidacy. If your child would benefit from a new activity or from participating in more extracurriculars, boarding schools will offer a myriad of options. If your student is learning the English language, immersion before college can be crucial.

But what if your student already has top grades and excellent study habits? If he is already dedicated to an activity and is achieving at a high level? Will boarding school help this student's college prospects? Maybe not.

Lucy was a student at a Fairfield County public school who was an accomplished lacrosse player—a member of a nationally ranked club team—who was invited to select national showcases. As a freshman, she was considering boarding school for her last three years of high school. Lucy and her parents were surprised that she was accepted to all the boarding schools she applied to, even those with small acceptance rates. It was clear from her contact with the boarding schools' lacrosse coaches that her lacrosse skills were what made the difference. Upon further reflection, Lucy's family decided to keep her home at her public school, where she could continue with off-season lacrosse practices with her club team. She was recruited by many colleges for lacrosse and committed to Yale in the fall of her junior year. It's safe to say that attending boarding school would not have improved her college options, since she was admitted to one of the most selective colleges in the world.

3

Campus Visits and Interview Preparation

The value proposition of a boarding school is its people. If you ask any student why they love their school, they will tell you that it's the community, including the teachers and students, that makes their school great. Boarding schools are more than just the buildings and the curriculum—it's the round-the-clock active lifestyle that makes them stand out from day schools. The campus visit and interview is your chance to look beyond the marketing materials and website and to evaluate the school and decide if it is a good match for your family. And likewise, the interview allows the admissions director to gain information and insight on your child as a candidate.

THE CAMPUS VISIT

At most schools a student and her parents are welcomed to campus for a tour and interview. These visits take place during admissions office hours, which are approximately 8:30 a.m. until 3:00 p.m. on weekdays. Many admissions office staff members coach sports or are involved with after-school activities, so appointments after 3:00 p.m. can be difficult to get. It's important to schedule interviews ahead of time, as appointments may be booked at popular times. Some schools have interviews and tours on Saturday mornings during the fall, which is helpful. Most are closed during the week of Thanksgiving, and many don't offer tours and interviews during exam periods or in the week before Christmas break. Interviews are offered from mid-September through mid-February for those applying for the traditional application deadline and at other times of year for students applying to schools with openings after the traditional application period.

Typically, each family is given their own tour guide: a student who is handpicked because of common interests or background. After about an hour of walking around campus and hearing from this student about her experiences, the family returns to the admissions office. The student has an interview with the admissions director, then the parents meet with the same admissions staff member, usually without their child, for a short parent interview. The final part of the visit is a meeting with an athletic coach or other special-interest representative. Students who would like to meet a coach can ask to do so, and if the schedules permit, it will be added to the visit itinerary.

When touring a boarding school, it's helpful to look beyond the grounds and facilities. Observe the people, and notice how members of the community interact with each other. If you are able to attend a sporting event or performance, or if you have the opportunity to eat in the dining hall, use these experiences to try to get a sense for what school life is like. Talk to students, staff, faculty, and parents. While you are there, consider the school's messaging. Do admissions staff and tour guides speak about accomplishments, awards, and successes after graduation, or do you hear more about connections between students, opportunities for growth, and student happiness? Do the students and staff seem happy and comfortable in the school environment?

INTERVIEW TIPS

You've read that boarding schools are all about community, and interviews are an important part of building this community. Just as the faculty and staff are interviewed before they can join the team, so are the students.

The interview is an important piece of the application process that is considered along with grades, testing, and teacher recommendations as a way to form a picture of the candidate, to learn what she is like and how she will contribute to the school community. A boarding school interview is a conversation. It is not a one-way conversation where the interviewer is asking the questions and the student is answering each one. Ideally, it's an exchange, and the interviewer will only have to ask a few questions to keep the conversation going.

Leave Cell Phones in the Car

Students should not look at their phones on the tour, in the waiting room, or in the interview, so it's best to avoid temptation and simply not bring a phone to a school visit. You could also hold your child's phone in your bag while on campus. A student admitted to me that he accidentally looked at his phone when he felt nervous during an interview, even though he had not intended to do so. Admissions deans say that they are disappointed to see applicants in the waiting room on their phones rather than looking at the yearbooks and publications in the admissions office or observing what's happening around them.

Introductions

When your student meets her interviewer, she should remember to stand up and shake his or her hand. She should look the interviewer in the eye and introduce herself. Teens today often use only their first name when introducing themselves, but in this more formal situation, a first and last name introduction is preferred.

At schools with a more formal dress code, such as a jacket and tie for boys, applicants should dress in a similar way. At schools with a casual dress code, it is okay to wear a casual but neat outfit, such as pants and a collared shirt, a casual dress, or pants and a sweater. Applicants should not wear jeans, workout clothing, or clothing that is revealing or distracting in any way.

Stay Focused

Students should try to make eye contact with the interviewer, and they shouldn't play with hair or jewelry.

Project a Positive and Enthusiastic Outlook

Remind your student that if he liked what he saw on the campus tour, he shouldn't be afraid to tell the admissions dean about it. Students should try to be positive in the way that they speak as well as show interest and enthusiasm about the school and their candidacy.

Send a Thank-You Email to the Interviewer

Be sure to take a business card or make a note of who interviewed your student. Contact information for each interviewer is on the school website. Applicants should send a thank-you email describing what they enjoyed about the visit or something new they learned from the conversation with the admissions dean.

VIDEO CONFERENCE INTERVIEWS

Schools also offer electronic interviews conducted either through Zoom or their own video conference system. While some schools only offer video conference interviews during their admissions office hours, others open up the schedule and conduct the interviews in the evenings, in the early mornings, and on weekends. This can be convenient for families who are concerned about missing school or work or for those who live far away and find it difficult to reserve time for school visits. One drawback of video conferencing interviews is that they are not as long as in-person meetings, and it may be harder to make a meaningful impression. Choate Rosemary Hall is one school that does not offer any in-person interviews and, out of fairness, requires all applicants to interview through Zoom. They do offer on-campus tours, but the interview part of the visit is done separately and from home.

DON'T SAY OR DO THIS AT AN INTERVIEW: TIPS FOR STUDENTS

Remind your student to consider the following behaviors as they prepare for interviews and campus visits.

Don't Criticize Your School or Any of Your Teachers

Remember to stay positive, since critical comments about your school reflect poorly on you.

Don't Discuss Activities That the School Doesn't Offer

If you are a swimmer but the high school where you are interviewing doesn't have a swim team, it is okay to talk about it as an activity that you have done, but don't spend too much time on it, and certainly don't tell the interviewer that you are hoping to join a high school swim team.

Don't Discuss Mental Health Challenges or Personal Relationships

It's best to leave stories about friendships, relationships, and personal situations out of the interview.

Don't Speak Poorly of the Boarding School

Don't tell them that you don't want to go to boarding school or that you prefer a different school.

Don't Answer Questions with One or Two Word Sentences

There are always students who will respond with "Good" and "Yes" to many of the questions, which makes it difficult to start a conversation. Look at them as conversation starters rather than questions.

Don't Pass on a Question or Decline to Answer

Take a moment to think, gather your thoughts, and answer the question in the best way that you can.

PARENTS INTERVIEW

Parents are often surprised to see that they will have an interview during the school visit as well. School representatives want to get a full picture of the applicant, and this includes getting to know the parents. The interview is a short discussion about the child and the families' reasons for considering boarding school. Admissions deans are on the lookout for parents who may be difficult or demanding, so be careful about controversial questions.

Questions for Parents

- Tell me about your child.
- What are your child's strengths and weaknesses? How do you hope his strengths will be developed? How do you hope her weaknesses will be supported?
- How did you learn about our school, and why would you like your child to attend?

- Do you have any concerns about your child being at boarding school or adapting to life here?
- What would you like us to know about your child that we have not asked?
- What questions do you have for me?

HOW TO PREPARE FOR THE INTERVIEW

Students should spend some time thinking about themselves, how they have grown, and what they would like to get out of high school. They should consider a few main points that they hope to get across in the interview. For example, a student who wants to discuss his summer volunteer work or his favorite English class should keep those thoughts close at hand and try to bring them up in the conversation if appropriate.

Questions for Students to Ask Themselves

- What have I contributed to my school or community?
- What are my strengths?
- What are my weaknesses?
- What do I hope to get involved with in high school?

It can be helpful to review interview practice questions since they can help students to think and reflect. For example, a student may be asked, "Why do you want to go to boarding school?" or another version of this question, such as "Why are you interested in our school?" It is important the students think critically about the reasons they give. Students should avoid vague answers such as "Because it is a good school." Instead, be specific. These are some common reasons for attending boarding school that can be used, in a student's own words, to explain his interest.

Why Boarding School?
- I would like a better education than my local schools provide.
- I want more of a challenge academically.
- I need learning support or help with my academic work.
- I want to do better in school.
- I hope to become more independent.
- I heard boarding schools have great teachers, and that is important to me.
- I want to meet students from all over the world.
- I hope to attend a school with lots of AP or other higher-level courses.
- I am impressed with the activities and sports offered at boarding school.
- I have a friend who has attended boarding school and told me good things.
- I talked to a coach from your school and liked what I heard.

While it is important to review the questions and practice with an adult in a mock interview, you should not seem rehearsed. Don't try to recall the answers that you had practiced. Remember that the interview is a conversation, and the questions are supposed to spark that conversation. And finally, relax and try to enjoy your discussion. The admissions officers are professionals who are used to talking to kids. Ryan Mulhern, director of admissions at St. George's, shares, "Our job is to make kids feel comfortable enough to share a little about themselves."

COMMON BOARDING SCHOOL INTERVIEW QUESTIONS

Interviews will vary based on the style of the interviewer. The best interviews are often the ones where very few questions are asked, and instead, a natural conversation occurs. Questions that may be used to start this conversation include the following topics.

About the Student's Current School and Life

- Where are you from, and where do you go to school?
- Tell me about your family.
- Tell me about a class you are enjoying.
- What are you doing in your science (or any subject) class right now?
- What are the qualities of an excellent teacher?
- Do your grades accurately reflect your abilities?
- When you are having trouble in a class, what do you do to improve?
- What is one thing about your current school you would change?
- Tell me about a book you have read recently? Who wrote it?
- What did you do last summer?
- What do you enjoy doing in your free time?
- What activities are you involved in either in school or outside of school?

About Boarding School and the Future

- What are you looking for in a high school?
- Why are you considering our school, and how have you gotten to know it?
- How do you feel about living in a dorm?
- Have you ever lived away from home, such as at sleep-away camp?
- What activities are you interested in getting involved with in high school?
- How can you contribute to our school community?

Other Questions

- What is the biggest challenge that you have faced in your life so far? How did you work your way through this challenge?
- What are you most proud of?
- Have you done any community service work?

- How would your friends describe you?
- What is an issue in the world that you are concerned about?
- What are your future plans and goals?
- What other schools are you applying to?
- What questions do you have for me?

Questions Students or Parents Often Ask

- Do students have advisors? How are they chosen, and when do they meet?
- Are students required to be on a sports team?
- How hard is it to make the sports team(s)?
- Are there classes on Saturdays?
- What are the hardest adjustments for new students?
- Do you have formal meals or any other time the whole school comes together?
- Do students have time to be involved with both sports and theater?
- What happens on weekends?
- Are there study abroad opportunities or school-sponsored trips?
- How many students enter in the ninth grade versus the later years?
- What is the evening study time like, and are teachers available?

Questions Parents Often Ask

- Is there a parent's association or other ways to get involved in the community?
- Who can I contact at the school if I want to know how my child is doing?
- If my child needs academic help, will they find my child, or does my child have to self-advocate?
- How can my child's special interest be pursued at your school?

- Do students have jobs or any duties at the school?
- When can parents visit campus?

Interview Questions from the Admissions Directors

Admissions directors often have a go-to question they ask every student or a favorite one they ask every year. I asked admissions representatives to tell me about a favorite question, one that they commonly asked this year, or to tell me about one of their more unusual questions. These are their responses:

- "Tell me about a time when something didn't go as planned. How did you handle this situation?"—Peddie
- "How would your friends describe you?"—Northfield Mt. Hermon
- "Define what a good community means to you," and "What is your superpower, and how will you use it here?"—Millbrook
- "Who is someone you admire and why?"—Mercersburg
- "Is there a question you wish I had asked you?"—Choate
- "Tell me about your friends. What do you admire about them? How would they describe you?" —Middlesex
- "What are you grateful for?" —St. George's
- "Have you ever held a different opinion from someone you love dearly?" and "If you had a million dollars, what would you do with it?" —Miss Porter's

INTERVIEW FEEDBACK

After the interview ends, the admissions officer will probably tell the student that she did a great job or that he enjoyed talking to her. He might say, "I could see you doing great things at our school." It's important not to read into these statements a sign of future acceptance. The interview is one part of the process, and it isn't until late January and February that the admissions committees start reading applications, shaping the class, and deciding who to accept.

I often get feedback from admissions staff members on how my clients performed in their interviews. It's surprising that most often, the parents and students leave the interview feeling great, and they will tell me that it went very well. But sometimes I hear a different story from the school. One boy confidently told me that he aced the interview, but my contact at the school said that the boy had answered the questions with just a few words, causing the interviewer to ask nearly twenty questions in an attempt to get to know him. Another admissions dean told me about how my client had taken several pieces of candy from the bowl on the interviewer's desk and eaten them during their discussion, which the interviewer found distracting. I heard about an applicant at an all-girls' school who told the interviewer that she prefers coed schools, a student who could not think of a book he had read recently, and several students who criticized their current school or teachers.

It's important to send an email thank-you note to your interviewer. At some schools the interviewer will send every applicant a thank-you letter either in the mail or by email. Communication between the applicant and the interviewer is encouraged and can continue throughout the application process. It's a good idea to give the interviewer an update in the winter about anything new that has happened inside or outside of school, such as improved grades, accomplishments in extracurricular activities, and honors or awards. Emailing the interviewer is a way to keep the dialogue going and to show your interest throughout the application process.

4

✣

Applications and Testing

The boarding school admissions process is detailed and time-consuming. It is the parent, not the student, who runs the process, completes most of the application(s), and makes arrangements for visits, recommendations, and testing. The one exception is the student essays, which should, of course, be completed by the applicant. The process described in this chapter is the norm for most of the boarding schools in the United States, although there are some schools with lighter requirements or different application processes.

INQUIRY FORM

The first step in the process is to complete an inquiry form for each of the schools you are interested in. This online form can be found on the admissions page for each school, and it includes basic questions about the applicant, including the home address, the school attended, and his activities and academic interests. When you complete the inquiry form, you are added to the admissions mailing list, which means you will receive notifications of events and deadlines. It also opens an account for you at the school so that you can register for an interview or campus visit and so you can send test results. For example, this is the link to Pomfret's inquiry form, which is found on their website, on the admissions page: https://pomfret.schooladminonline.com/portal/new_inquiry.

APPLICATION

Rather than completing an individual application for each school, applicants use a "common" application that is completed once and then can be sent electronically to multiple schools. There are two options: the Standard Application Online, called the SAO (https://www.admission.org/services/standard-application-online-sao), with four hundred member schools, and Gateway to Prep Schools (www.gatewaytoprepschools.com), which has sixty member schools. While there is some overlap, many schools are only part of one of the two application systems, meaning that students may have to complete both Gateway and SAO in order to apply to all the schools on their lists. For example, a student applying to Avon Old Farms, Portsmouth Abbey, and Choate would use the SAO for the first two schools and Gateway for the last.

The first step when using Gateway to Prep Schools is to complete part 1, which includes basic information about the student and parents, a checklist of schools where the applications will be sent, a detailed activity list, and a short answer section about academic and personal achievements. Once this part is complete and the application fee is paid, it is submitted to the schools. At that point, the rest of the Gateway application becomes available. This includes the sections for student essays, parent essays, and a recommendation.

Like the Gateway application, the SAO asks applicants to complete the profile, which includes biographical information, including a list of interests and achievements, and it allows students to upload a multimedia file, which could feature a musical performance, a sports event, or participation in another area of interest. After this first section is submitted and the fee is paid, students can then add specific schools to apply to and begin work on their essays.

STUDENT ESSAYS

I recommend that parents discuss the essay questions with their child and help them decide what to write about. For example, when asked about a book he has enjoyed recently, an eighth grader should not write about *Diary of A Wimpy Kid*, which is intended for younger readers and not known to be challenging. Parents can remind their child of other books or even suggest new ones to read before he or she writes the essay. Once the essay topic is decided, the student should write independently, with only minimal help with editing. It's important for the writing to be the student's own thoughts, in his or her own voice.

On the SAO, applicants are asked to write one essay of 250 to 500 words, but they can choose from among six different prompts. In addition to this main essay, the application asks students to complete all of the following shorter prompts, with each response ranging between 200 and 250 words:

- Aside from books or articles assigned for school, what book(s), article(s), podcast(s), and or documentary(s) have you enjoyed most in the last year and why?
- Describe *either* an academic/extracurricular achievement *or* a challenge that had a meaningful impact on you. What did it take to accomplish the achievement or overcome the challenge, and what did you learn from that achievement?
- Each person has unique characteristics that define who they are. Choose three words that best describe you as a person, and explain how they represent you.

On the Gateway to Prep School application, each school has its own essay questions. Some are detailed, such as the question from Berkshire, which asks students to create their own winter term class, or the one from Groton, which asks how the student's community has shaped who he is today.

Students applying to several Gateway schools will have many short answers and essays to write. For example, a student applying to seven schools on Gateway may have as many as eighteen or twenty short-answer questions and essays to complete. I recommend putting all the questions on a Google Doc and completing them there, taking the time to review and edit before pasting them into the application.

PARENT ESSAYS

Parents get the opportunity to have their voices heard during the application process too. I recommend parents use anecdotes and examples rather than descriptive adjectives to make their points. The parent statement questions include the following:

- What are your hopes for your child in their secondary school experience?
- Describe an experience that posed a significant challenge for your child.
- In the years ahead, where do you see the most room for growth in your child?
- What qualities of your child's character and mind most delight you?

MULTIMEDIA SUBMISSIONS

One way to present your child's interests and accomplishments is through a video submission. Athletes create short videos with game highlights, which are similar to what is used in recruiting at the college level. Dancers and musicians can prepare a piece just for the purposes of the video, or they can use excerpts from their performances. Visual artists showcase their work in a video or through slides, often including five to ten pieces. Creative writers or journalists can create a short portfolio of unpublished or published work. In addition to these uses, many boarding school applicants submit casual videos to let the admissions team learn more about them. In this age of content creators and with the popularity of short videos, it's not surprising that many teens use this opportunity to submit something creative and interesting. Admissions deans say that they enjoy the creative video submissions, and they are often watched by multiple staff members. Examples of creative videos I have seen include one that follows a student and his puppy that is training to be a guide dog, a video that showcases a student's baking talents, and one that includes an applicant's commentary on a trip to an exotic location. The videos can be submitted on the SAO or Gateway application. Some students upload their work to YouTube and distribute the link to their interviewer, coach, or teacher. Not all applicants have a multimedia submission, but if your child has a talent or passion to share visually, creating a video can be helpful to the application process.

GRADED ESSAY

Many schools require applicants to submit an essay written for school, such as an English or history paper or another piece of analytical writing. Students should save the paper as a PDF and then upload it to the SAO or Gateway application. It's not required that the paper have an actual grade on it, since many students receive their grades electronically rather than with the grade written on the paper by the teacher. The admissions directors understand this and will accept the paper with or without the grade on it. Some applicants attend schools that rarely assign papers, asking instead for journal entries, presentations, worksheets, or projects. If a student has no paper to submit, he should ask his teacher to assign him a paper just for the purpose of his boarding school applications. One common suggestion is to write a short analytical piece about a book from English class. Admissions directors at selective schools want to admit students whose writing is on grade level or above and will be able to thrive in the reading- and writing-heavy curriculum.

RECOMMENDATIONS

Recommendations are often the most insightful part of the application since admissions deans know that it is the one piece that parents and students have no control over, and in fact, because the letters are confidential, parents and students never even see them. The application requires that students submit recommendations from their school counselor, their current English and math teachers, and an optional third teacher from any subject area. They can also submit an optional special interest recommendation from a coach, music teacher, youth group leader, employer, or someone else who knows the student well. Teachers are asked to wait until at least October to write the recommendations so that they have time to get to know the student. It's important to note that these recommendations are not just letters or narratives that teachers write; they are actually forms that use ratings and an evaluation of personal characteristics and academic promise.

Teachers are asked to rate students in twenty-seven different areas, including problem-solving skills, reasoning, academic achievement, academic potential, willingness to take academic risks, concern for others, and the ability to work independently. They additionally ask for the child's overall recommendation, first as a student and then as a person. The teachers are asked to check one of these options for each category:

- One of the top I have ever encountered
- Excellent, top 10 percent this year
- Good, above average
- Below average
- No basis for judgment

Teachers also write a narrative about the student and answer questions such as these:

- How well does the student write in comparison with other students whom you have taught? Please be specific about areas of strength and weakness.
- How well does the student accept advice or criticism?
- Please comment on this student's character, citizenship, and contributions to your community.
- Please add any additional information that will give us a more complete picture of the student.

School counselors submit a form that includes an attendance and disciplinary report, as well as information on the school grading system and course offerings. The counselor is given a space to write about the student and his contributions to the school, but the admissions deans understand that at many schools, the counselor does not know the students well, so the lack of insightful comments will not be held against the student.

TESTING

Although standardized testing has been an important part of the boarding school application process for decades, it has now become optional at many schools. Applicants should check the testing requirements at each school they are interested in before developing their test prep plan. But just because a school doesn't require testing doesn't mean you should not take the test. For students who are good test takers or who have the time and motivation to prepare for a test, a strong test score can be a helpful part of their candidacy. Students who have learning disabilities or an individualized education plan (IEP) at their current school that allows for extra time on tests or assignments can apply for extra time on their Secondary School Admissions Test (SSAT) or Independent School Entrance Exam (ISEE) test.

The SSAT (www.ssat.org) includes reading, verbal, quantitative, and writing sections. Students in grades 8 through 11 are given the same test, but scores are calculated on a percentile based on each student's grade. For example, an eighth grader earning a score of the eighty-fifth percentile knows that he scored at the same level or higher than 85 percent of the eighth graders who took the test. A tenth grader will get a percentile score comparing him to other tenth grade students. Therefore, the eighth and tenth graders taking the same test may have the same raw score but different percentiles scores. It's primarily the percentile score that is used in boarding school admissions.

The writing section is not graded but asks the students to write a short essay based on a single prompt. The sample essay is sent with the grade report so admissions deans are able to see the complete, proctored writing sample.

Students can take the SSAT remotely at home or at a testing center, or they can take a paper and pencil version of the test on a select Saturday at a local independent school.

Although the SSAT is the most commonly used test for students applying to boarding schools, there is another option called the ISEE (https://www.erblearn.org/families/isee-by-erb/). It is similar to the SSAT, with sections in math, verbal, and reading, as well as an essay. Students usually decide which test to take before they start their prep work.

Students applying for the upper grades of high school or the PG year do not have to submit SSAT or ISEE scores. They can submit a PSAT, ACT, or SAT test score, which is convenient since they can also be used for college admissions. The PSAT is given at most high schools in October of sophomore and junior years, which is good timing for those students applying to boarding schools.

Test Prep

Students taking the SSAT or ISEE should spend some time familiarizing themselves with the test and reviewing the core concepts. Practice and review can help students to increase their scores. I recommend working with a tutor, who can provide targeted lessons and review to help a student improve. While it's not always possible to find an in-person tutor in your local area, there are national tutoring companies that have trained SSAT and ISEE tutors available to work through video conferencing. Test Innovators (www.testinnovators.com), the leader in test prep for SSAT and ISEE, offers an inexpensive subscription that includes access to actual practice tests, as well as problems and test prep strategies. Customers can also arrange to work with Test Innovators tutors for an additional fee.

Other Testing

Students applying to boarding schools with learning support programs are not evaluated by standardized tests but are instead asked to send their neuropsychological exams. This testing measures cognitive ability, such as the Wechsler Intelligence Scale for Children (WISC) / Wechsler Adult Intelligence Scale (WAIS) tests, which are often used to diagnose ADHD or a learning disability. The results of these tests help the school learning center staff make a plan for support.

FREQUENTLY ASKED QUESTIONS ABOUT BOARDING SCHOOL APPLICATIONS

It's April and past the deadline, but can my child still get into boarding school?

Yes! While it may seem that the boarding school admissions process has a rigid and inflexible timeline, many of the schools are welcoming to families who are late in getting started. It's only the most elite and selective schools that fill their classes in the spring. With the exception of those schools, the majority of the other boarding schools throughout the country will accept "late" applications. Families who start making inquiries in March or April will find plenty of schools to visit and many openings. By the summer many schools are full, and it will be more difficult—but not impossible—to find an opening for September.

My son really needs to make a change this year. Can he start boarding school immediately?

Yes! There are many schools that enroll new students in January, and there are some that will start a new student when their fall term ends in late October. The most selective schools never accept new students midyear. Schools that add new students midyear will only consider it when there is an open spot, which may be due to a student leaving midyear or to the school not reaching full enrollment in the fall. The best way to find out which schools will enroll a new student midyear is to call schools of interest to ask or work with an educational consultant, who will have an understanding of admissions trends and openings.

Should my son stay in touch with his interviewer?

Yes. Your student should send a thank-you email to the person who interviewed him or her, who is most often a member of the admissions team but is sometimes a teacher or an alumnus. If you have new information to share after the application has been submitted or if you want to reiterate your interest in the school, it's okay to follow up with the interviewer.

A coach is recruiting my son and encouraging him to apply. Does that mean he is getting in?

Not necessarily. Some coaches are active in reaching out, but for schools that are selective in admissions, it takes more than the approval of the coach.

My daughter's application is in by the deadline, but the teacher hasn't written the recommendation yet. What should I do?

The schools will not discard your application as incomplete if it is missing a recommendation. The deadline is generally for the applicant, and teachers are given more time if needed. An email reminder to the teacher about the missing recommendation will usually get things back on track.

My daughter is not a "joiner," but her grades are very good. Since grades are the most important part of the process, she will do fine, right?

Not necessarily. At selective schools, they have many students with strong grades. What really stands out is a student who is a good student but who also is accomplished in another area or has the potential to be a leader in the community. With schools offering so many sports, arts programs, and clubs, admissions committees are looking for students who will get involved and make a positive impact. Joiners do have an advantage in selective school admissions. Students who are not involved in activities inside or outside of school may have trouble getting into selective schools despite their strong grades.

5

✧

Financial Aid and Scholarships

The high price of boarding school leaves many parents wondering whether they will be able to afford this opportunity for their child. They see the large tuition fees, often around $75,000 a year, along with assurances from the schools that a large percentage of families receive financial aid and that the average aid award is actually quite meaningful, often over $50,000. But they also know that applications for aid often exceed the school's scholarship budget. Parents are left wondering, What does this mean for me? Will I get a financial aid award? And will it be enough? Are there merit scholarships that aren't based on my family's finances? Are all boarding schools priced the same, or can I find a less expensive option? These are the questions parents should be asking as they build their school list, apply for financial aid, and consider their child's future for high school and beyond.

BOARDING SCHOOL COSTS

Although there is a range of prices, the majority of boarding schools had tuition rates between $65,000 and $75,000 a year in the 2024–2025 school year. At the high end of the range is IMG Academy, which offers an academic program with elite athlete training for the cost of $92,000 a year, as well as Forman School, which offers a college prep program with learning support for $91,000. Ross School costs $86,200 for domestic boarding and is one of the higher-priced traditional schools. The lowest-priced boarding school is St. Lawrence Seminary High School in Wisconsin, which offers a boarding program for boys for only $17,300 for the 2024–2025 school year, including room and board.

Schools that charge tuition between $70,000 and $79,000 a year include many names families recognize most: Taft, Choate, Kent, Canterbury, Salisbury, Hotchkiss, Suffield, Lawrenceville, Stevenson, Western Reserve, Asheville, Middlesex, and St. George's, among many others. This price includes tuition, books, room and board, activity fees, and almost everything else a student needs for her life on campus.

Schools that have slightly lower tuition, with costs hovering around $65,000–$69,000 a year, include Phillips Exeter, St. Paul's, Groton, Phillips Andover, Shattuck St. Mary's, St. Stephen's, and Army and Navy, among others.

Schools with domestic boarding tuition in the $50,000–$60,000 range include Cranbrook, Cheshire, St. James, Linsley, Baylor, Tallulah Falls, Indian Springs, and San Marcos, among others.

While these tuition rates may seem high, it's important to note that the cost of tuition is less than the funds needed to educate a student. The budget for the expenses of the academic and extracurricular programs, campus maintenance, teacher salaries and health benefits, dining hall operations, and the many other aspects required to keep a school running successfully typically exceeds the tuition revenue. The schools rely on donations from parents and alumni, as well as fundraisers, to cover the extensive costs in their budgets. All enrolled students are therefore subsidized by donations, as the tuition their family pays does not cover the full cost of educating them. For example, at Andover, the annual tuition is $69,600 for boarding students, but "the full average cost to educate a student at Andover will exceed $85,000 [that] year," according to a letter to parents.[1]

If these school tuition prices seem high, what are your options? You can consider need-based financial aid, merit scholarships, or low-cost boarding schools.

NEED-BASED FINANCIAL AID

I get more questions and uncertainty about financial aid than any other topic in boarding school admissions. Unlike with college admissions, there is no online financial aid award estimator that allows you to input your financial information and get an aid estimate in just minutes. Parents aren't sure if they will qualify for aid at all, and if they do, they don't know if it will be enough to make it work. Even well-off parents wonder if they can qualify for some aid to offset the high boarding school costs before facing years of college tuition.

A high-income father said to me, "My son wants to go to boarding school, but I don't want to pay a lot. We need to cover his college, and we have a lot of other expenses. If they give us a good aid package, he can go, but we are not going to stretch for this."

But one of the things that I have learned about financial aid over the years is that it often does ask the family to stretch, and it asks them to stretch a great deal.

The Salisbury School website includes a relevant point about aid that is common to most boarding schools: "As a simple principle, every family makes a financial sacrifice, commitment and investment when their son attends Salisbury School."[2]

Boarding schools do not typically give middle-income and higher-income families a deal that is so good they can't turn it down. But these families may be given a financial aid award that allows them, with sacrifice, to make the boarding school option work for their family. Full-tuition scholarships are sometimes awarded to families who have both low income and low assets, but those grants, which often include laptops and travel expenses, are competitive to get. Let's consider what the schools review when giving these awards.

FINANCIAL AID APPLICATION PROCESS

Parental income is the biggest factor in the financial aid evaluation, followed by assets and other considerations, such as where you live, how big your family is, and how many other children are in tuition-charging schools and colleges. The boarding schools evaluate this information by reviewing both the applicant's tax filings and financial aid application.

There are two third-party financial aid forms used by most of the boarding schools: School and Student Services (https://www.solutionsbysss.com) and Clarity (www.clarityapp.com). Clarity is the service most commonly used, and their application takes just a half an hour to complete. Clarity removes the need to upload tax returns and W2 forms by transferring them directly from the IRS. The application asks questions about whether a family rents or owns a home, how many cars are owned, how much they spend each month, and whether both parents work. The financial profile of each applicant is scrutinized, and then an *expected family contribution* is determined. The scholarship grant amount is supposed to be the total cost of tuition, minus the expected family contribution. But schools often use the Clarity expected family contribution as a starting point in aid deliberations and will make their scholarship award after considering the financial aid budget as well as the needs of returning students and others in the applicant pool. This means that a boarding school may ask a family to pay more than the amount that Clarity decides a family is able to pay.

Divorced or separated parents must each complete a form. They are confidential, and one parent will not be able to see the other parent's responses or financial statements. A student cannot qualify for aid without both parents participating or without certification that they only have one parent in their life. The financial aid award will give one expected family contribution, which does not determine how much each parent should pay.

FINANCIAL AID AWARD AMOUNTS

The size of the financial aid award received by a student is dependent on their family's financial need and, to some degree, on the schools they apply to. At Lawrenceville, where tuition was $79,500 in 2024–2025, 34 percent of students got a financial aid award. The average aid award is $60,000, meaning that the average family on financial aid paid just $19,500 for their Lawrenceville education. It's interesting to note that 15 percent of the awards go to higher-income families making between $250,000 and $325,000, although their awards were certainly smaller than the average.

At Phillips Andover, a strong financial position and large endowment allows them to be among the most generous with financial aid. It's Andover's seventeenth year of *need-blind admissions*, which means that the school will meet 100 percent of demonstrated financial aid for each admitted student. By the numbers, 45 percent of Andover students receive financial aid, with an average grant of $43,000.

George School has a large financial aid program, which accounts for 25 percent of the school's operating budget. The school will meet 100 percent of demonstrated need, and it awards aid to 50 percent of their students. George is unique because they give such extensive need-based aid but also offer partial merit scholarships, which are given without a financial aid application.

Episcopal High School, with an annual tuition of $72,000, breaks down its financial aid awards on their website in a way that is helpful to parents who are trying to understand how much they will be asked to pay. As you can see, Episcopal

Table 5.1 Financial Aid at Episcopal High School, 2023–2024

Gross Family Income	No. of Families	Avg. Family Contribution
Under $39,999	21	$820
$40,000–$69,999	20	$1,765
$70,000–$99,999	25	$7,564
$100,000–$149,999	21	$17,342
$150,000–$199,999	24	$26,141
$200,000–$299,000	29	$33,162
Over $300,000	21	$44,742

Over 35 percent of the student body receives financial assistance. The average grant offered to families is $51,430.
Source: Episcopal High School website (https://www.episcopalhighschool.org/admissions--aid/costs--financial-aid)

enrolled twenty-one students who paid, on average, only $820 a year. Table 5.1 represents Episcopal High School but also is a model to consider potential aid levels at other schools, as many schools have similar financial aid distributions.

FINANCIAL AID TIME LINE

Parents should complete the forms through the Clarity app by February 1 of the application year. It's important to meet the deadline since students applying after the deadline are only rarely considered for financial aid.

While a few schools are need blind and won't consider your financial aid status in admissions, there are a great many schools that do. These schools may have large financial aid budgets but many more requests for aid than they can manage. This means that students who are not applying for aid, who we call full-pay students, are often at an advantage in the admissions process. When I work with students applying for financial aid, I ask them to apply to additional schools, as they are likely to get more wait lists and denials than a similar student without financial need. Even though so many students receive financial aid, there are many who are disappointed.

Families in need of tuition assistance must apply for financial aid during a student's first year at boarding school. Some parents feel that it is easier to get admitted if they don't apply for financial aid, so they decide to pay for the first year of tuition and apply for financial aid in subsequent years. However, most schools do not allow this strategy and only give financial aid to returning students who have applied before—unless there is a material change in their financial situation.

LOANS

Grants and family savings are the best way to fund school tuition, but sometimes, there is still a shortfall. Families often turn to loans to cover the excess costs. It's important to be cautious about loans, especially if you will need to take on debt for college tuition. If you decide loans are required, the first thing to consider is a payment plan offered through your boarding school. Many schools allow parents to spread the payments out over ten months. Parents who need a loan can contact their bank or consider an education loan company, such as Your Tuition Solution (https://www1.yourtuition solution.com/), which specializes in private school loans.

MERIT SCHOLARSHIPS

Families who don't qualify for need-based financial aid often wonder if they can fund a boarding school education through merit scholarships. There are a few opportunities for full-tuition scholarships, but they are competitive. The more common merit scholarships offered are grants from $5,000 to $20,000, which reduces the tuition costs but still leaves a sizable amount for the family to pay. It's important to note that many of the boarding schools that are need blind and known for generous financial aid, such as Andover and Exeter, do not offer any merit scholarships, since the school philosophy is to use scholarship money only for those with need.

Families looking for merit aid should research schools of interest and consult the tuition and financial aid page of their websites. Schools that award partial merit scholarships include Avon Old Farms, Chatham Hall, Christ School, Dana Hall, EF Academy, Fountain Valley, George, Gould, Grier, Hargrave, Madeira, Mercersburg, Miss Porter's, Peddie, Perkiomen, Pomfret, Rabun Gap, Ross, Salisbury, Suffield, Williston Northampton, among many others.

Schools that offer full-tuition merit scholarships include Baylor, Cranbrook, Culver, McCallie, Mercersburg, Peddie, Pennington, and Western Reserve.

At McCallie the full-tuition scholarship is called the Michaels-Dickson Scholars Program, and candidates are judged not only on academic success but also character and demonstrated leadership. Culver Academy offers a full ride, including tuition, room and board, uniforms, a computer, and a summer experience to sixty-two distinguished scholars each year. Pennington offers two scholarships for each incoming class, and Western Reserve's full-tuition scholarship is awarded to a student who is curious about the "human collision between art and science."[3]

The Caroline D. Bradley Scholarship is awarded by the Institute for Educational Advancement, a nonprofit dedicated to gifted youth.[4] Applicants must start the application process during seventh grade to be considered for enrollment in ninth grade. The rigorous portfolio application process includes a review of grades, testing, recommendations, essays, and a student's creative work. Last year, fifty-one students made it to the finalist round where they had in-person interviews with the scholarship committee, and twenty-seven students were awarded the multiyear full-tuition scholarship. The award can be used at any school in the country, either a boarding or day school, although the scholarship does not cover the room and board part of the tuition fees.

LOW-PRICED BOARDING SCHOOLS

Families looking for a bargain-priced boarding school can consider one of the many schools with tuition and room and board priced at under $45,000 a year. Schools in this price range may not have the extensive facilities or offerings that the more expensive schools have, but they offer the opportunity for an active community and a strong academic program. Many of the military schools, such as Valley Forge, Hargrave, Fork Union, and Missouri Military Academy, are in this price range, as are schools such as Florida Prep, Oak Hill, Scattergood Friends, St. Bernard's Prep, and Subiaco.

Another type of low-cost boarding school is a religious day school that has a small boarding component. Most of the boarders are international students who are working to achieve English fluency and benefit from an American education. For example, St. Bede Academy, a Catholic school in Illinois, has 240 day students, 38 international boarders, and 3 domestic boarders. Tuition and room and board in the 2024–2025 school year was only $37,000. Other similar schools include Cotter School in Minnesota, Michigan Lutheran, Wisconsin Lutheran, St. Stanislaus in Mississippi, Maur Hill in Kansas, St. Croix in Minnesota, and St. Lawrence Seminary in Wisconsin.

FREE BOARDING SCHOOLS

Most people don't realize that there are free boarding schools in the United States. The majority are public boarding schools, funded by the state, but there are also three independently run, free-tuition schools. Regarding the public boarding schools, some states cover all of the costs, while others ask families to pay for the cost of room and board. A few of the schools are for eleventh and twelfth graders only, while most enroll students in the full high school experience, including grades 9 through 12. Students are required to be legal residents of the state at the time of the application and during school residency.

Public boarding schools include Alabama School of Math and Science, Alabama School of the Arts, Illinois Math and Science Academy, Maine School of Science and Math, Mississippi School for Math and Science, Mississippi School of the Arts, North Carolina School of Science Mathematics and Science, North Carolina School of the Arts, South Carolina Governor's School for the Arts and Humanities, South Carolina Governor's School for Science and Mathematics, the Seed School of DC, and Oklahoma School of Science and Math.

Two boarding schools were founded for disadvantaged children to benefit from a residential community and strong academic program. Milton Hershey School in Pennsylvania was founded over one hundred years ago to offer a tuition-free education to low-income children. The deed of trust left by Catherine and Milton Hershey funds the entire program, which includes the option for year-round housing, clothing, medical care, and graduate support. The campus houses two thousand students and includes an ice hockey rink, an equestrian center, a television studio, and free admission to Hershey Park. Girard College is a school in Philadelphia that offers boarding five days a week, with students going home on weekends. It is a tuition-free school for low-income children with single parents.

Eagle Rock School in Estes Park, Colorado, is a free boarding school that is a corporate responsibility initiative of American Honda Motor Company. The school is thirty years old, enrolls about seventy-five students from across the United States, and has a professional development center, in addition to a college prep program. The school is open to students from families of all income levels. Eagle Rock is open to accepting bright students who have not been successful in a traditional high school.

ACCESS TO EDUCATION PROGRAMS

Organizations that offer a guided path to boarding school are referred to as *access to education programs*. These nonprofits are committed to providing access to a quality education for low-income students and to students of color. In many cases, the programs don't provide financial support, but they guide students through a high school preparation program and then assist with the application and financial aid process. Most of these programs are regional—for example, a student must be a resident of New York and a member of the Boys' Club of New York in order to benefit from their private school program, and NJ Seeds is only for residents of New Jersey. However, organizations like A Better Chance offer a national program of support for students applying to independent schools. The following is a list of various organizations that offer access programs:

A Better Chance: www.abetterchance.org
Boys' Club of New York: www.bcny.org
Breakthrough New York: www.btny.org
Daniel Murphy Scholars: www.dmsf.org
Harlem Lacrosse: www.harlemlacrosse.org
Hartford Youth Scholars: www.hysf.org
High Jump Chicago: www.highjumpchicago.org
Inspiring Young Minds: www.iymglobal.com
Jack Kent Cooke Foundation: www.jkcf.org
New Jersey Seeds: www.njseeds.org
Oliver Scholars: www.oliverscholars.org
Prep for Prep: www.prepforprep.org
Reach Prep: www.reachprep.org
Teak Fellowship: www.teakfellowship.org
Wight Foundation: www.wightfoundation.org

6

Inside the Admissions Committee

The concept of an admissions committee is an intriguing one. It's a group of professionals who spend many weeks evaluating, judging, and collaborating with each other to shape an incoming class. Whether it's admissions for colleges, law schools, business schools, or boarding schools, the decisions at very selective schools are often shrouded in mystery, leaving applicants to wonder if there is a secret sauce or a preferred path to their desired school. Let's examine what happens in the boarding school admissions deliberation session and how decisions are made.

WHAT THEY ARE LOOKING FOR

When asked what the committee is looking for in an applicant at St. George's School, Ryan Mulhern, the director of admissions, said, "Academic success. We are looking for kids who are already achieving."[1] And with one thousand applicants for about one hundred new student spots, St. George's has the ability to be that selective. Like most of the elite boarding schools, St. George's is looking for students who will come to school ready to excel in their academic life.

The applicant pool at top boarding schools is dominated by students who have straight A or A– grades. One admissions director told me that in reviewing his applicant pool, it was "rare to find more than one B or B+" on the transcript, then went on to say, "We have seen new levels of grade inflation."

Another admissions director from a selective school said, "We have to look beyond grades. Teacher recommendations can be helpful. We like to look at quantitative strength, since kids who struggle in math struggle everywhere."

Admissions committees don't make decisions based on grades alone, but they consider the applicant in the context of the school he attends, evaluating the whole academic picture. Another admissions dean told me, "We look at distance traveled. How far has this student come? How much did she do with what her environment provided?"

Another area that is important to admissions committees is participation and engagement. Mulhern from St. George's said that they are looking for students who will be involved in campus life. "We have twenty-six sports teams, a play, music groups, and so much more, and we need kids to participate and lead these activities. We will accept some kids who are generalists and can do a lot of things on campus, as well as those who are specialists and do one thing really well."

Doug Price, director of admissions and financial aid at Middlesex School, agrees: "We expect our students to do a lot of different things and don't make them choose between the arts and athletics. We had three sports team captains with major roles in the school play this year."

And while academics and involvement in student life are two important aspects of the boarding school application, character and personal characteristics are also key factors. Many school admissions brochures and websites mention these important elements of the applicant evaluation. For example, at South Kent School, the admissions webpage says, "In addition to being able to find success in our curriculum, we are looking for individuals who have the desire and ability to be contributing members within our community."[2]

And at Blair Academy, they are looking for "high character individuals, first and foremost." They seek to enroll students who are "kind, caring, bright."[3]

Price from Middlesex echoed these priorities when he discussed the three themes that his school considers in admission: curiosity, character, and engagement:

> We look for curiosity—students who want to learn and who have demonstrated intellectual curiosity in their lives. We look for evidence of character, which includes kindness, resilience, and respect. Engagement is important to us. We are a place that expects a lot of interaction between students and faculty, and we want kids that will interact in the classroom and be involved in all aspects of school life.

Demographics is another factor in admissions, as schools need to keep their gender balance and class sizes at the levels that work best for them. They have a plan in terms of how many students they want to enroll in each grade for each application year. For example, the Blair admissions newsletter states that they plan to enroll thirty-five boys and thirty-five girls in the ninth grade, fifteen boys and fifteen girls in the tenth grade, five girls and five boys in the eleventh grade, and five boys and five girls in the PG year.

COMMITTEE DISCUSSIONS

An admissions associate at a selective school that accepted fewer than 15 percent of applicants told me about their process for reviewing applicant files and welcoming a new class. "Every file is read by three associates, which includes the staff member who interviewed the student and parents. The applicant is graded on four attributes and can receive a point for each," she explained, and highlighted the following categories.

Personality

Is the student a person of good character? Does he participate in class, and is he a positive school community member? Is this a student who I would want in my dorm? The grade for personality is related to these questions and is decided through the interview, teacher recommendations, and essays.

Verbal

This score is based on the student's grades in English and history, her SSAT reading and vocabulary scores, and the English teacher's recommendation.

Quantitative

This score covers math achievement and is determined by his grades in math classes, SSAT math score, and math teacher's recommendation.

Impact

The student gets an extra point in the process if he can make an immediate impact at the school, such as starting on a varsity team as a freshman or having a leadership role in a school play or music group. The admissions associate further explained, "An impact point is also given for students whose parent or sibling attended the school, if they have the potential to be a big-time donor, or if they are an American student from outside the New England or New York and New Jersey area. A point is given for diversity, and for a student who brings something that the school needs, which could be a boy who has experience singing and performing in musical theater, or an impact player for a sports team."

* * *

Once these three evaluators have graded each student in those areas, it is time to make decisions. Students with low scores are clear denials, and students with high scores are clear acceptances. It is the large group in the middle that moves to the admissions committee for further discussions. They discuss these files focusing on academic readiness and the ability to make an impact on student life. By the end of committee negotiations, the class has been set and offers extended, with families given one month to decide whether to accept the offer. At this time, the admissions team shifts gears away from evaluating, and they begin marketing again, trying to "yield" their accepted students, or in other words, get them to enroll.

At St. George's School, they use a rubric in evaluating applicants. Points are given for academics, teacher recommendations, the SSAT score or graded essay, the interview, extracurricular activities, and the effort on the application. St. George's has an admissions committee of eight, and they discuss all applicants thoroughly. They consider opinions from coaches who have been in contact with applicants. They look to create a diverse class in terms of cultural and racial balance, geography, and public and private school background. The St. George's admissions team reviews the multimedia submissions from the application, which is often used for sports highlight reels and music auditions. Ryan Mulhern suggests that only about 30 to 40 percent of applicants send a video (which is an optional part of the application), but it's not only the athletes and musicians. He has seen students submit videos about their day, about scuba diving, and about all sorts of creative things they are interested in.

Teacher recommendations are valued at St. George's. "A good recommendation can really help a kid," Mulhern said, "Especially if they really know the student." But he also acknowledges that there are many submissions from teachers who don't write any comments, preferring only to check off the boxes, which doesn't add insight. These evaluations won't hurt applicants, but they are a missed chance to learn more about the student.

At Middlesex, nine admissions officers review the 1,300 to 1,400 applications that arrive. They narrow it down to 300 potential admits, then move to the difficult cutting phase, admitting only 200 applicants to get to 115 to 120 matriculants. Each application is read by at least three people. In January the committee meets, and every applicant is discussed. For applications that are easily determined to be acceptances or denials, the discussion is short, but some cases merit over twenty minutes of discussion in committee.

Middlesex rates candidates on a scale of 1 to 5 in the categories of academics, personal attributes, athletic or arts contributions, and an overall rating. Usually, the ratings of all three admissions officers are consistent, but sometimes they aren't, which is what leads to a lengthy discussion.

FIRST-CHOICE LETTERS AND ADVOCACY CALLS

As a consultant and a high school placement counselor at a K–8 school, I schedule calls each January with admissions directors at the schools to which my students have applied. We discuss my students, what they are like, how they will fare in boarding school, and how I think they will contribute. It's interesting that every call includes the question, "Where are we on their list?" The admissions associates are asking directly about how my client sees their school and where it is ranked on her school list. It can be a difficult question in some cases. I worry that telling the admissions associate that his school is not my student's first choice will hurt that student, and I also worry that telling him she is a sure thing and will accept an offer could make them more comfortable to wait-list her since they know she will agree to attend later. So why talk at all?

These conversations between the schools and the educational consultants, access program counselors, and high school placement counselors at K–8 schools are called *advocacy calls*. The calls are a common part of the admissions process for students who work with an advisor. The schools want to know more about the students, and they may ask an open question like, "What is his superpower?" Or they may ask a specific question about a grade or a comment on a teacher recommendation. But the question "How does the family feel about us? Where are we on his list?" is the most complicated one.

I recently worked with a student named Anika, who had applied to eight boarding schools: Choate, Groton, Taft, Exeter, Andover, Hotchkiss, Deerfield, and Lawrenceville. In my role as her secondary school counselor, I reached out to all of the schools to discuss Anika and her candidacy. Three of the schools never responded to me, but I had conversations with staff members at the other five schools. Mary, an admissions associate at one of the schools, was excited about Anika and asked good questions about her. I knew that Mary's school was one of Anika's top choices, so I told her so. Mary seemed interested and said, "Anika is reading well, I expect her to move on to the next round."

Two weeks later, I got an email from Mary that said, "I wanted you to know that we are going into some difficult rounds of shaping this week. If you have any up to the minute yield information on Anika, we would like to know. Unfortunately, we will be cutting 165 files this week, and we want to know of any students for whom we are their top choice and yield is guaranteed."

I quickly went to Anika's parents to ask them again if they had a first choice. They indicated that they did, it was Mary's school, and they had already emailed their interviewer to tell him it was Anika's first choice. Hearing that, I contacted Mary to reaffirm that her school was indeed Anika's first choice.

Just a day later, I received an email from a different school on Anika's list. It was a friendly note asking if I knew if that counselor's school was Anika's first choice. And since I could only report to that counselor that no, they were not Anika's first choice, I decided not to respond at all.

A few days before the March 10 notification date, I received another email from Mary, this time with disappointing news.

"Unfortunately, Anika didn't make it into our 'accept' group. We're giving her a waitlist, but I'm not expecting it to move forward since our 'accept' group is pretty committed."

I knew that Anika was very close to being accepted, but since this school had an acceptance rate of under 15 percent, there were many strong candidates who were denied. On March 10, Anika's family was disappointed to receive a wait list from Mary's school.

I was surprised to hear that Anika was accepted at just one school out of the eight she had applied to, receiving wait lists and denials at all the others. The school that accepted Anika was the one with the counselor who had emailed me asking if it was her first choice, which I didn't respond to, since it was not at that time. Anika ended up enrolling at that school and loved her experience there. Of the admissions process, Anika's mother said, "Anika ended up at the perfect school for her. Deciding on the first choice didn't really matter in the end."

It goes to show that giving a first-choice notification to a school is a nuanced situation that doesn't always have the intended impact. Some families feel that their candidacy will be enhanced if they send a *first-choice letter*, which is an email indicating that their child will enroll if accepted. But most admissions directors who I spoke to discourage this practice. "Don't bother with a first-choice letter," said Ryan Mulhern of St. George's. "We are trying to build the best class we can, but we also want the kids to find their best fit." Another admissions associate told me, "[We] discourage first choice letters. We don't want to put pressure on families to make this decision before having the opportunity to revisit." A third admissions director told me, "We will look at a first-choice letter if we get it, but we only get about ten a year, so it isn't a big part of our process."

WAIT LIST

Many parents are surprised to learn that at selective boarding schools, more applicants are wait-listed than are accepted.

The large wait lists include students from across the applicant pool, as it's unknown which types of student will be needed to come off the wait list. If they didn't get enough ninth grade boarding girls, they need to look at the wait list for this group. Didn't get enough musicians? No soccer players? They can look to the wait list to help shape the class.

At St. George's, they typically deny about 830 applicants, wait-list 350, and accept 170, with a goal of about 100 new students. Likewise, at Middlesex, they receive about 1,350 applications, deny 800 of them, accept 200, and wait-list 350, with a goal of 120 new students. Those 200 students who received acceptances from Middlesex and the 170 who received offers from St. George's probably received offers from other schools as well, and they will attend Revisit Days to help them make a decision. The schools work hard to showcase their school on Revisit Day and to connect with accepted students.

The students on wait lists are fully qualified and received high ratings from the admissions committee. In fact, many of the denied students also received high ratings and would have been successful at boarding school, but with limited spots and a competitive applicant pool, there are many strong candidates who are disappointed. Some parents are encouraged by their child getting wait-listed and wonder what they can do to turn it into an acceptance. Sometimes, they call the school immediately on March 10 or 11 to show their interest, or they consider asking for additional teacher recommendations or having their counselor or someone from the school call on their behalf. But it's important to know that the wait list doesn't move until some of the accepted students turn down their spots. Typically, this doesn't happen until April 9 or April 10, since families often use the full month to make their decision, or they do decide early but then fail to notify the other schools that they won't be taking the offer. There is a lot of angst among wait-listed students, who wait and wonder what they can do to help their case. The best thing they can do is let their interviewer or admissions contact know that they plan to remain on the wait list and that their interest is still strong.

When the reply date of April 10 arrives, some schools will not get as many deposits from new students as had been expected, and they will go to the wait list to give offers. By this time, most of the wait-listed students have moved on and accepted other offers. A school that gave three hundred wait-list decisions may find that only fifty are still active and interested in being considered after April 10. They look through the small group of students still hoping for a place at their school and make offers to those who fit the criteria they are looking for. Students who are accepted from the wait list usually have a short time to make their decision—in some cases, only a few days, and in other situations, a full week or two. St. George's was like many schools that did not end up going to their wait list at all this year, since their projections on yield turned out to be accurate.

CASE STUDIES AND RESULTS

Case One

Ashley was a ninth-grade girl from Maryland who attended a well-regarded suburban public school. She played on a nationally ranked lacrosse team and had been named to several national and regional select teams. Ashley had a big personality, was outgoing, and involved in other sports and clubs. Ashley's parents considered boarding school since she was having some conflict with girls at her school, and they liked the idea of the busy school community that leaves less time for social media. Ashley contacted lacrosse coaches at all of the schools she applied to and was in touch with them throughout the year.

> **Grades and testing:** Ashley had all A's and A–'s and an eighty-first percentile SSAT score.

The schools: Ashley applied to Taft, Choate, Lawrenceville, and Deerfield.
The results: Ashley was accepted at all four schools.
Summary of feedback from the schools: "We see Ashley as someone who would thrive here. Her lacrosse accomplishments made her stand out, but we also liked her friendly personality and commitment to academics."

Case Two

Sam was an eighth-grade boy from a private school in New York. He had a passion for music and theater and attended a New York City intensive weekend music program. Sam had acted in a small role in a Broadway show. He sent a video of his singing and acting to the schools he applied to and connected with the theater teachers.

Grades and testing: Sam had 3 B's and 2 A's in his core classes and an SSAT score in the eighty-second percentile.
The schools: Sam applied to Exeter, Deerfield, Choate, and Northfield Mt. Hermon.
The results: Sam was accepted to Northfield Mt. Hermon, denied at Exeter, and wait-listed at Deerfield and Choate.
Summary of feedback from the schools: "He was close, but his grades were lower than our typical accept, and the teacher recommendations had lower ratings for classroom participation and community engagement."

Case Three

Anna was an eighth grader at a private school in New Jersey who was involved in everything her school offered. This included playing on three sports teams, acting in the school play, and participating in the math team, the broadcast news club, and a studio art club. She was not exceptional in any one activity, but she was a good teammate and community member. Anna's parents wanted her to go to a top boarding school but knew that the chances were not high, so they decided to apply to eleven schools.

- **Grades and testing:** Anna had all A's and A–'s in her core subjects during seventh and eighth grade and had an SSAT score of the eighty-eighth percentile.
- **The schools and results:** Anna was accepted at Taft, Kent, Miss Porter's, Peddie, and Tabor. She was wait-listed at Choate, Exeter, Deerfield, Loomis Chaffee, and Hotchkiss. She was denied at Andover.
- **Summary of feedback from the schools:** "We liked Anna a lot, it was just such a competitive applicant pool that she didn't make it all the way to an acceptance."

Case Four

Brian was a sophomore at a high school for gifted students in Nevada. As a child, he was diagnosed as profoundly gifted, learning to read at age two and understanding math and science concepts with ease. Brian enjoyed independent projects, such as assembling computers, studying astronomy, and reading about topics of interest. He was on the school soccer team but had no other school involvement. Brian's parents wanted him to go to boarding school to take advantage of advanced classes and to encourage him to socialize more.

- **Grades and testing:** Brian submitted an SAT score of 1420, which was lower than expected for a profoundly gifted student, but since the test hadn't interested him, he hadn't focused on it. His grades in core subjects included two C's in freshman year and one C in sophomore year, with the other grades in the A range. His father explained that Brian wasn't interested in grades and often missed assignments, but he could easily get high grades if he would try.
- **The schools:** Brian applied to Choate, Andover, Exeter, and St. Paul's.

The results: Brian was denied at all four schools.

Summary of feedback from the schools: "His grades are simply too low. Plus, I don't see much involvement outside of school, and his teacher recs rated him very low on teamwork and participation, so it's a clear deny for us."

Case Five

Carter was an eighth grader at a public school in New Jersey. He was a member of his town soccer and basketball teams, and he played the drums in the school band. His parents noticed that Carter's grades declined from A's to B's in middle school, and he often complained about going to school. They did a neuropsychological exam to test for learning disabilities and discovered that he had ADHD, but no other areas of concern. Carter began to see an executive functioning tutor, who helped him with organization. His parents felt that he had so much potential but just wasn't reaching it at his current school. They wanted to find an environment where he would be engaged and involved, where he could be happy and do well in school.

> **Grade and testing:** Carter didn't take the SSAT and applied without testing, instead sending his neuropsychological exam.
>
> **The schools:** Carter applied to Trinity Pawling, Cheshire, New Hampton, and Tilton.
>
> **The results:** Carter was accepted at all four schools.
>
> **Summary of feedback from the schools:** "Carter had a great interview and seemed excited about getting involved in sports and music here. His neuropsych exam shows that he is very intelligent but needs support in a few areas. We see Carter as someone who would do very well in our program, and we hope he joins us next year."

7

✛

Is Boarding School the Right Choice?

Parents will know a lot more about boarding schools at the end of the application process than they did at the beginning. The school visits, interviews, online research, and family talks on long car rides between campuses have a way of helping parents and children understand what the boarding school experience is about and whether it is right for them.

THE DECISION

On March 10, the notification date for most boarding schools, the decision will arrive through an email, or it will be updated in the admissions portal. There is a moment of suspense when students log in to find out their result, which is either an acceptance, a denial, or a wait list. The acceptance will bring congratulations and invitations to Revisit Days, while the denial is a short letter offering best wishes for your future at another school, and the wait list means you are still under consideration.

Accepted students have until April 10 to make a decision on whether to enroll. By this date they should accept the offer from one school and turn down all the other schools that gave them an offer. As a consultant, I often have to remind parents to let the schools know that they won't be taking the offer. They sometimes feel that they only have to accept the offer they want, with no need to get back to the schools they won't be attending, but it is an important courtesy to notify a school immediately if your student won't be attending.

EVALUATING YOUR CHOICES

Presumably, you have applied to schools that are a good fit in terms of academic profile, extracurricular offerings, campus culture, and location. At this point in the process, deciding between several good options can be difficult. I encourage families to do additional research and make an educated choice. Most often, the final choice is made based on the community, the people, and the general feel of the experience. But it is important to look at the schools closely, trying to understand if your values match the school culture and if you feel confident about the faculty and the structure of student life at the school. After all, you are leaving your child in the care of the staff members at the boarding school. They, in partnership with you, will be going through milestones and experiences with your child during their years at school. You want to make sure that you chose well.

Most schools offer a Revisit Day, which includes panel discussions, tours, workshops, lunches, and other events to celebrate the accepted students and to help them make their final decision. I encourage families to ask questions of staff members, students, and parents at these events, sometimes asking the same question of different people.

Each family may have their own area of interest that they will focus on. For one parent, it may be about getting to know a sports coach to get a sense for how much playing time their child will get, as well as what the culture of the team is like. Another may be interested in diversity and evaluating how many students and faculty of color are on campus, while another parent may be considering whether all voices are truly welcome on campus, including those with conservative views. Some families may be evaluating the arts program, looking both at the facilities and the course offerings. Other parents are most interested in asking about social media and gaming restrictions or how evening dorm life is conducted to help keep students off of screens.

Parents and students evaluating the academic program of a boarding school can look at the course of studies but should also consider a document called the School Profile. Nearly every high school in America, public or private, writes a three- to four-page document that is sent to colleges with their students' applications. This document is useful in comparing schools since it includes information on courses offered, AP, SAT, and ACT scores, college placement, and demographic information about the students. It's also helpful to use when comparing local public and private school options with your boarding school choices. Some schools keep their School Profile private, but others post it on their website, on the "College Counseling" page.

Speaking with other parents is a good way to get to know a school community. You may meet parents of current students at Revisit Day, open houses, sporting events, theater performances, or through a connection arranged by the admissions office. Some schools offer a direct email connection to current parents on their website so you can reach out to parents easily and immediately.

PROBLEMS AT BOARDING SCHOOLS

Boarding schools are not immune to the problems plaguing society today, such as sexual abuse, drug and alcohol use, bullying, and mental health issues. Parents can ask about a school's support for students who are suffering from mental health issues, and they can ask how bullying or student conflict is handled. Some schools have a one-strike policy for alcohol usage, leading to an immediate expulsion, while others allow for a learning experience and penalty on campus. Drug use almost always leads to an expulsion. Parents can ask school representatives about their policies and experiences in these areas.

A few boarding schools have had incidents of sexual abuse that have gone to trial or have been well publicized. An internet search with the school name and terms such as "lawsuit" or "sexual abuse" can help parents learn more about what occurred and how the school responded. Some of the cases are recent, but the lawsuits are often decades old and involve faculty who are no longer at the school. While we can learn from the past and gain insight into school culture and responses, it's most important to evaluate the current school leadership and current policies.

WHEN STUDENTS LEAVE BOARDING SCHOOL VOLUNTARILY

Not all boarding school placements go well. The following stories show situations that ended with parents withdrawing their children from their boarding school. Their stories show a side to boarding school life that isn't included in the marketing materials or on Revisit Days but are important to consider when evaluating if boarding school is right for your family.

* * *

Jack applied to six selective boarding schools and was disappointed when he was denied by all of them. He was a student with A's and B's and a sixty-fifth percentile SSAT score, and although he played many sports, he wasn't playing at the level where coaches would be interested in talking with him in the admissions process. His application was not strong enough for Deerfield and Hotchkiss, his two top choices. Jack's parents sent a late application to a school that a family friend attended as a day student, and Jack was admitted.

Located nearly four hours away from Jack's home, the school had one hundred boarding students and five hundred day students. It seemed to have the best of both worlds—a large and vibrant community with so many options for sports, academics, and working with a diverse group of students, along with a small and nurturing boarding program. At Revisit Day, Jack and his family toured the dorms and got to know the residence life staff and were impressed with all that they saw. The school was very selective for day students in the area, but the admissions standards were lower for domestic boarders, as they received fewer applications from this demographic. Jack's parents realized that this was a good opportunity for their son to attend a top-tier, well-regarded school, which was what they had wanted for him all along. Jack's freshman year went well, and his parents were proud to see him thriving academically and participating in a sport every season. Although there were weekend activities for the students, by the end of the year, Jack had started to spend most weekends at the homes of his friends who were day students.

By the middle of sophomore year, Jack was with his day student friends every weekend, sometimes even after school. Jack's parents felt uneasy about him spending so much time with other families. They had imagined him as part of a boarding community, but instead, it felt like he was living far away from home with various other families, hopping from one house to the other. One Saturday night, after midnight, Jack's mom noticed an Uber receipt from a ride her son took near his school. When asked what happened, Jack answered that he was at a party, and the parents of his friend had fallen asleep. With no ride home, Jack decided to use his Uber account. His parents were upset with the situation, both because he was out so late at a party and because the family hosting him was not supervising him to a level with which they were comfortable. Jack's parents refused to allow him to sign out to go to a friend's house the next weekend, which made Jack angry. They allowed him to sign out for the next few weekends and tracked his location from his phone. They were disappointed to find him out past midnight at various locations in the suburbs. The parents chose not to reenroll Jack for junior year, moving him to their local public school instead.

* * *

Aiden was a baseball player who was admitted to a well-known, selective boarding school. He had strong testing and grades in the B+ range, but he was in need of executive function support. Before deciding to enroll their son, Aiden's parents talked with the learning support team, and they recommended tutoring sessions in the fall to help him adjust to school life. He had an ADHD diagnosis, but because his SSAT testing and grades were strong, the school had no concerns about his ability to handle the rigorous coursework. This school offered very little learning support, since they generally did not accept students who needed extensive academic help. Aiden's parents considered enrolling him at a school with a true learning support program but didn't feel it was in Aiden's best interests to turn down an elite school that had accepted him.

Aiden was hit hard by the workload as soon as he started on campus. He had trouble managing his homework assignments, waking up on time, and remembering items for class and practice. As the weeks went by, he became anxious and worried. Aiden's parents reached out to his advisor, dorm parents, and teachers, trying to arrange support.

He received some support, but by midyear, Aiden only seemed to do worse, missing assignments, falling behind, and becoming more anxious and unhappy. In January of his freshman year, Aiden's mother rented an apartment near campus, and he finished the school year living with her. She was able to create the structured environment and support that he needed to get through the school year. Ultimately, Aiden's parents decided that it was not the right school for him and did not reenroll him for sophomore year.

* * *

Some students leave boarding school for social reasons, after a conflict with friends, romantic interests, or classmates. Others leave because of homesickness, a change in the family financial situation, or the desire to go back to their local high school and hometown friends or club sports team.

WHEN STUDENTS LEAVE BOARDING SCHOOLS INVOLUNTARILY

When I visit boarding schools, one question I like to ask of students and faculty members is "How many students have been asked to leave this year and why?" In years past the most common reasons have included drinking and drug use. While those infractions still happen, we now see more dismissals due to cheating, including plagiarism, and the misuse of social media and texts. When evaluating schools, some parents ask about the discipline policy and whether they are a "one strike and you're out" type of school or whether they work with students who have infractions.

* * *

Anna was a driven and high-achieving girl who was also an accomplished violinist. She had never had anything but As, and her violin video impressed the admissions teams during the application period. She enrolled in a well-known boarding school with rigorous academics and a strong music program. Her adjustment to academic life at boarding school was easy, but keeping up with her music practice proved to be more difficult. Anna was used to practicing violin no less than two hours each day, and although the school had music practice rooms, she had trouble finding the time in her busy day for the violin, which was not only her area of talent but also her time of solace and relaxation. Early in her first semester, she stayed in the violin practice room and missed her soccer practice. The next semester, she was late for sports practice and dorm check several times. Feeling the academic crunch, she lied to her advisor, saying that she had three tests in one day, then asked for permission to take one of the tests a day late. These infractions led to Anna being dismissed from the school.

In the boarding school world, very few students are actually expelled. Typically, the parents are told of the infraction and given the opportunity to withdraw their child from the school before the discipline hearing. In Anna's case, the school told her parents that because of the lying and the number of infractions during the year, it would likely lead to an expulsion. If she withdrew on her own, she would not have to report it on her college applications as an expulsion. Anna withdrew and returned to her local public school.

* * *

Matthew was an active and involved student at a New England boarding school where he played two sports, was the editor of one of the campus newspapers, started a stand-up comedy club, and served as a dorm proctor. Matthew was devastated to be dismissed in October of his senior year. It was difficult to return to the public school that he had left so long ago, and he worried it would have implications on his college applications.

Matthew's first strike was that he was caught drinking, along with ten other students, on a warm night at the start of his senior year. Three weeks later, he failed to report a boy and girl who were alone in a dorm room; they should not have been there, and Matthew had tried to cover for them. These infractions were serious enough to the school that they recommended that he withdraw before disciplinary hearings would lead to his expulsion. It was difficult for Matthew and his parents to accept that these infractions, which would not have existed if he had attended a day school of any kind, would so negatively impact his future.

* * *

Tori was a sophomore at an East Coast boarding school where she thrived socially and academically. However, she was dismissed for cheating. Girls in her dorm had a collection of old tests and papers, and Tori copied significant parts of one of the papers into her own work. The teacher recognized it and placed her on probation. A few weeks later, Tori had a disagreement with another girl and wrote critical things about her in a group text, which was later forwarded to the dean of student life. And finally, there was another cheating incident, where Tori was accused of looking up information on her computer during a test. Tori and her parents were advised that she would likely be expelled if she went through the discipline hearing process, so they chose to withdraw her immediately.

PARENTS SAY: THINGS THAT SURPRISED ME ABOUT LIFE AT BOARDING SCHOOL

- "There is such a family vibe on campus. There are dogs and kids everywhere! My daughter's school has over thirty dogs living on campus with faculty members, which makes it feel so homey."
- "I thought I would feel my son's absence more, but we actually have a stronger relationship now that he is at boarding school. We have better interactions, and he talks to us more than he did when he was at home."
- "My daughter is 'known' at school, and that's a great feeling. The teachers and students all know her, and she feels like she is a part of something great."
- "Teens take ownership of their everyday decision making at boarding school. This leads to maturity and growth, which you can see almost immediately in your student!"
- "I didn't expect to meet other parents of my daughter's classmates, but through the parent's committee and meeting at games and performances, I have gotten to know

some of them really well, which makes us feel connected to the school."
- "I was surprised at how much time the English teachers spend on the papers, writing comments and helping them become better writers."
- "My son was always so quiet and a little lost in his large middle school, so I was happily surprised at how many friends he has made at boarding school."
- "Like any high school, there is drinking and vaping. I had hoped there wouldn't be."
- "My son spends time gaming at night after lights out. I didn't expect this, and I'm not sure what they can even do about it, but it's a problem."
- "I didn't realize how unsupervised they would be at times. They have many hours of freedom on the weekend days. I had sort of assumed they would know where she is at every minute."

II

THE WORLD OF BOARDING SCHOOLS

8

Life at Boarding Schools

Community and connection are a big part of boarding school life, and for many families, it's their biggest selling point, as it provides a high school experience they are not able to find at home. Screens can dominate teen social life, whether they are gaming, watching TikTok, or communicating through Snapchat or text. Even teens who do socialize in person often feel that something is lacking in their social life. They want school spirit, fun activities, and mixing with teens beyond their immediate friend group. Many kids today are looking for more social engagement, deeper interpersonal interactions, and more fun. When I tell my clients about weekend life and traditions at boarding schools, I notice them perk up and listen carefully. Everyone wants to be part of something bigger than themselves, as well as to feel a sense of pride and belonging. Many teens find that and more at boarding school.

MATRICULATION

Even move-in day is filled with tradition. If you go to Peddie, you and your parents will drive onto campus for the first time and be welcomed by cheering students, ringing cowbells, and waving signs that say, "Welcome Falcons!" Students are immediately engulfed into the community as upperclassmen help them find their dorm, unpack, and meet their classmates.

Miss Porter's School has many honored traditions, several of which are kept confidential and only revealed to girls once they begin their experience at Porter's. Their Welcome Tradition, also called "German," is one of the most cherished of these traditions. It's a formal ceremony that has been held for many years, and it is a unifying thread that all Porter's alumni, called "ancients," experience as they are welcomed into the community. Many of the details are only known to the girls who have participated in it, but Sarah Quinn, director of admissions at Miss Porter's, calls Welcome Tradition "magical and so special," and describes it as having some theatrics around it, music, and use of German words and songs.

New students at Proctor Academy attend a wilderness orientation, where they spend four nights camping in New Hampshire's White Mountains. They travel in a group of eight students and two faculty members, hiking, swimming in mountain streams, setting up camp, and preparing their own food. Students are challenged, and they discover new strengths, forge a bond with their group, and begin the school year sharing a common experience with their classmates.

At Hotchkiss, new students go to the chapel for a ceremony that welcomes them to the community. They introduce themselves to their classmates, shake hands with the head of school, and write their names in a historical leather book. On the last day of orientation, Hotchkiss students participate in a tradition called the contra dance, which is a square dance in the field house that has the whole community spinning their partners on the dance floor. At Choate, entering students attend a matriculation ceremony, casually called "signing the register," where they sign a statement pledging themselves to "personal growth, integrity, self-discipline, and caring for others."

On their first day at Culver Academy, students walk through the Logansport Gate entrance to the school, where they are welcomed by the head of school, the commandant of cadets, the dean of girls, and the top student leaders. The matriculation tradition at boarding school makes students feel welcomed and invested as an important part of the school community.

DAY IN THE LIFE

A day at boarding school is a busy day. Students can sleep later than their public school counterparts since classes start around 8:30 a.m. and they have no commute time. They hurry off to the dining hall, where they either eat a full breakfast or grab something quick to go. The morning is busy with classes and an advisory period or morning break, followed by a hearty lunch, which is often reported as a favorite time of the school day. Some East Coast schools have a half day of classes on Wednesdays and Saturdays, which allows their sports teams time to travel long distances for away games at other boarding schools. Going to school on Saturday mornings may seem onerous, but most students adjust quickly to it and enjoy the midweek half day.

When classes end, students go right to a structured activity period. This means sports or other student activities. Dinner follows soon after, and then students may have a club meeting or free time before study hours start, typically at 7:00 p.m. Evening study time is an important part of boarding school life, and one which is managed differently from school to school. Most boarding school students are allowed to study in their rooms, sign out to meet with a teacher, or work with a study group in the library. Freshmen or those on academic probation may have to work in a proctored study hall. At some schools, phones are taken away during study hours, and teachers walk through the dorm to be sure students are working. After study hours end, often at 9:00 p.m., students may continue with their school work, or they can go to the campus snack bar or visit friends in other dorms. They must return to the dorm by the sign-in time assigned to their grade. At some schools, the Wi-Fi is shut off at night to ensure a good night's sleep for all.

At Hargrave, students turn in their phones on Sunday nights and spend the academic week without them. They are able to focus on school, sports, and activities, and they are more fully engaged and involved. Hargrave supplies fishing poles, bicycles, and other things to keep the boys active during the week. Although the students are eager to get their phones back on Fridays, many admit that the time without the phone better allows them to focus academically and connect with classmates. Buxton is another school that is shaping its school culture with a limit on electronics and screen time, which allows students to be present and pursue activities and interactions with students and faculty without the distraction of a smartphone. Although flip phones and noninternet-based electronics are permitted, smartphone use is limited at Buxton.

WEEKEND FUN

Callie, a student at Kent School said, "The best thing about Kent is that everybody goes to things. No one stays in. We go to games, we go to the bonfire, we stay up late and talk in the dorm. It's so much fun here!" Weekend life at boarding school is active, and while students have academic and sports or club obligations, they have plenty of time for fun and relaxation.

At Avon Old Farms, a recent weekend activity schedule included a Friday night bus trip to Walmart, Five Guys Burgers, and a movie theater. The Saturday night schedule offered a trip to a go-cart center and dinner at a restaurant, as well as options for students staying on campus that included open gym, open ice, a college football game–viewing party in the Hawks Nest Student Center with wings and pizza, and a pickleball tournament. The Hawks Nest includes big screen TVs, a snack bar, and games, and Avon students are allowed to invite guests from the local girls' schools. At Millbrook their student center is called the Barn, and it is used as a daily hangout spot, as well as for dances with DJs and fun theme parties.

Masters School, which makes good use of its location near New York City, offers trips to see Broadway shows, the New York City ballet, Knicks basketball games, and visits to street fairs and tourist attractions.

Priyanka, a student at Peddie School,[1] said,

> I love to spend my weekends on Saturday Night Activities, more commonly known as SNAs. These activities vary from mall trips to whitewater rafting. I love these trips because they have created so many common experiences and memories for me and my friends. One example would be when my best friend and I went whitewater rafting together. I learned so many things about her and her past experiences with the ocean. The Broadway trips are always a highlight of my year. Being able to go see plays on Broadway with my friends is always so much fun! Every bus ride back, my friends and I listen to the soundtracks of the musicals and debrief about what we thought of the show. On the days that I decide not to go on an SNA or Broadway trip, I stay and hang out with my friends. Even if I don't leave campus, there's always something to do, and I have done so many activities that are just as fun as going off campus. With gingerbread house–building competitions, karaoke nights, and Find A Teacher (a hide-and-seek game where the teachers hide and students seek), I never find myself bored on campus.

Lucie, a student at Northfield Mount Hermon (NMH) said, "There is this school dance called Spring Jam, and I love it because the key thing about this dance is that the faculty gets to spray liquid paint on the kids. And it glows in the dark, so you'll be dancing and getting attacked by paint, and everyone is glowing."

Charlotte, a student at Cate, said, "My favorite part of boarding school is weekends with my friends. We like to go to the pool and do homework or go into the local town,

Carpinteria, and get brunch at a coffee shop. Sometimes we will go to the beach when it's warm or head to Santa Barbara to do some shopping. One really fun time I had at Cate was when my friends and I organized a friend group tennis tournament at our campus tennis courts with our guy friends. We split ourselves into teams, brought music, and had a big tennis tournament. It was so fun!"

Lucie from NMH described fun things she likes to do on campus: "After class, my friends and I will go into the forest and make our way to a secret waterfall that is located in the middle of nowhere, but it's such a peaceful place to be away from everyone. My second favorite part of the day is dinner. I love my school's dining hall, with the chandeliers and the wooden tables and chairs. I will sit down and have a two-hour dinner every night with all my friends. We talk about many things and are always the loudest in the dining hall. We all get to catch up about how long and tiring our day was, and we get to chat with the sweetest dining hall staff."

Eliza, a student at Westminster, said, "My favorite part of the day is simply hanging out with my friends. Just talking and laughing in someone's room after a hard day relieves a lot of stress and is what I will look back on most fondly."

Every school seems to have a competition between dorms, which takes place on a special weekend. It's not only sports events but dorm video competitions, airband performances, a cheer competition, and silly games like pillow polo, egg toss, water balloon toss, or tug-of-war, among others. More serious competitions include Kent's Extreme Wiffle Ball League, which ends the championship game with food trucks and music for all students to enjoy. Students at Hill School enjoy Javelin Ball, or J-Ball, which is like baseball but played with a tennis ball and racquet, allowing fielders to "peg" the base runner with the ball to get them out. McCallie students enjoy a serious game called Battleball, which is similar to dodgeball. At Westminster they play Stickball and host a tournament with customized T-shirts and a Stickball trophy for the winning dorm.

TRADITIONS AND CEREMONIES

Traditions, customs, and ceremonies are what bring boarding school students together in a shared sense of experience and community. Whether it is celebrating Chinese Lunar New Year, Headmaster's Holiday, the excitement of the first snow, or enjoying a day of competition with a rival school, boarding schools know how to mark the occasion and how to celebrate it.

Headmaster's Holiday is a spontaneous day off that is celebrated by students at many boarding schools across the country. At Groton School, where it is called Surprise Holiday, Sophie Zhu, a student writer for the *Circle Voice*, writes about this special day off, where part of the fun is in the announcement: "Senior prefects work hard to make the announcements extra special. Prefects brainstorm extraordinary ways of announcing the holiday—some notable examples include circling the school in a helicopter, popping out of a trash can wearing green, and waving green flags from the roof of the Schoolhouse."[2] The announcement is made during the morning meeting, and students are welcomed with donuts before they board buses to take them for a day in Boston or Cambridge. The winter version of Surprise Holiday is announced in the evening so that students can sleep in on their day off.

Charlotte, the student at Cate, described her school's special ceremony for seniors:

> Sunset Ceremony at Cate happens twice a year. It is an event in the evening in which the entire student body and faculty line up, and the seniors go down the line and give them all a hug. The first one happens at the beginning of the year and is sort of a way to welcome the seniors into their final year, wish them luck, and have them make contact with everyone. The second one happens at the end of the year and is much more emotional. It is right before seniors graduate and is a way for everyone to say goodbye, wish them well, and celebrate them.

Arts Weekend at St. Andrew's School in Delaware is jam-packed with opportunities to showcase students in the arts. They have ensemble performances, an orchestra concert, a play, film screenings, an art show, literary readings, and a dance showcase, which are admired by students and their parents. St Andrew's also has a tradition of an all-school trip to Washington, DC, where students meet with alumni in their places of work while also visiting museums and cultural sites together.

At Mercersburg Academy, Irving-Marshall Week is their most beloved tradition, dating back to the school's founding. Every student at Mercersburg is a member of either the Irving Literary Society or the Marshall Literary Society, which have their own colors and mascots. At the end of the winter term, campus is decorated with banners, and the two societies square off for five days of volleyball, dodgeball, basketball, foosball, board games, video games, and other contests. On the final night, a speaking contest known as declamation features five students from each society who take the stage in front of the entire school and perform monologues they have memorized. Judges evaluate and score the declaimers for content and delivery. The winning society is announced later that night at a school dance, and spring vacation begins the next morning.

The spring semester at Berkshire includes Mountain Day, a day when faculty and students enjoy the time off to explore the outdoors, as well as the spring carnival and the Green and Gray Ball. Berkshire also hosts a fun game of chaos and competition called Last Bear Standing, which involves the entire school in a game of tag with the players eliminated until one winner is left.

The Tapping Ceremony at Kent School is a special way to introduce the school's new prefects and senior council members. The whole school gathers for the ceremony where the seniors "tap," or pick, the next year's student leadership. Only a few faculty members know who will be tapped, so when it happens, it's a fun surprise that makes the students cheer. After the Tapping Ceremony, Kent hosts a bonfire and party for the entire school.

At Middlesex, wood-carved plaques are displayed around the school, created by graduates as far back as 1901. They serve as a social history, as you can see what was important to students during different eras of the last century. Today every senior is required to carve a plaque, and there is an art class to help them as they document something about their life at Middlesex.

GAME DAY AT BOARDING SCHOOL

Boarding school sports rivalries are intense, spirited, and fun. Game day is not just a football game but, typically, a whole day with all the fall sports teams competing against each other. Andover and Exeter have the oldest rivalry in high school sports, competing against each other three times a year, once for each season. At Deerfield, on the night before their rivalry day with Choate, they have a pep rally, bonfire, and chants and cheers before the entire school comes together for the games. At Episcopal High School, Spirit Weekend is a celebration of "the Game" against Woodberry Forest, which is the oldest football rivalry in the South, played every year since 1900. Events at Episcopal include the Spirit of the High School Dinner, the Maroon and Black Ball, and tailgating before and after the Game. Woodberry Forest has a pep rally and a Bonfire Bash that is open to students, parents, and the whole community. The game itself draws a crowd of alumni who have a deep emotional tie to these schools, as well as happy students and parents enjoying school spirit at its finest.

> **GREAT BOARDING SCHOOL SPORTS RIVALRIES**
>
> Andover vs. Exeter
> Choate vs. Deerfield
> Peddie vs. Blair
> Hotchkiss vs. Taft
> Baylor vs. McCallie
> Episcopal vs. Woodberry Forest
> New Hampton vs. Tilton
> Hill vs. Lawrenceville
> Loomis Chaffee vs. Kent
> Groton vs. St. Mark's
> St. George's vs. Middlesex
> Holderness vs. Proctor
> Fork Union vs. Hargrave
> Eaglebrook vs. Cardigan Mountain

DINING AT BOARDING SCHOOL

The dining hall is the heart of the campus at boarding school. And while most meals are hosted cafeteria style, with students joining friends and sitting together, there is a unique boarding school tradition of formal dinners, where students are asked to mix it up with seating assignments to help them get to know others in the community. This tradition has different names, procedures, and details at different schools, but the goal is the same: to build community and share a meal with people from outside of a student's friend group. It often involves getting dressed up in a jacket and tie or dress and enjoying a properly set table (with a tablecloth), and it sometimes includes a special meal, announcements, or singing.

Parents at Deerfield wrote about how their daughter did not like the idea of sit-down dinner, saying, "Being forced to sit at a table with random students she did not know? Not happening!"[3] At Deerfield, round tables include ten students and two faculty members. Two students per table are assigned to serve and must arrive fifteen minutes early to set up and bring platters of food. It is one of the few schools that has a formal dinner seven nights a week, and it is seen as a core part of school life. The dean of students welcomes the group of over six hundred diners with the words "For food, for friendship, for the blessings of the day, we give thanks. Amen."[4] On Sundays the dinner ends with the students standing, sometimes putting their arms around each other, and singing "Evening Song," which is Deerfield's cherished anthem.

The parents who wrote about their reluctant daughter continued, "Her initial impression of the value of the sit-down dinner changed almost immediately. She came to appreciate and enjoy the opportunities presented by Deerfield's dinner tradition, deepening her understanding of how shared history and traditions contribute to a feeling of living in a supportive family environment. This, and it was actually fun!"[5]

At Episcopal High School, they call it "seated dinner," and it takes place on Wednesday nights, while at Cate School, it is called "formal dinner" and happens a few times a trimester. It's called family-style lunch at Westminster and happens four times a week, while St. Andrew's School of Delaware hosts family-style meals on Wednesday nights, with students taking turns as waiters, both serving and clearing the tables. Formal dinner is a popular tradition at many boarding schools, but there are also holiday banquets and "bus meals" for athletes traveling to games. Additionally, at McCallie, an all-boys school, they have "fourth meal," which is a hearty 9:30 p.m. snack served in the dining hall after study hours.

JOBS AND SERVICE LEARNING

Students in boarding schools get real world experience through service learning, unpaid jobs on campus, and internships. Every boarding school offers opportunities for community service, and students often do these projects together as a dorm group or as an athletic team project. Some schools have unique internship or campus jobs programs that give students valuable hands-on work experience. These jobs can help students realize it's the little things they do that can impact others in a meaningful way.

At Deerfield Academy, community service can be a student's cocurricular commitment, which is done during the time that athletic teams practice. These students can serve on-site four days a week at locations including animal shelters, nursing homes, after-school programs, or food distribution centers. Outside of that regular commitment, Deerfield students can participate in one-time community service events on the weekends. Singing groups perform for the elderly, sports teams work with local youth, and dorm groups participate in a variety of activities to help the community. Deerfield offers grants to support students in their work to help others.

At Madeira School, the cocurricular internship program offers students the unique opportunity to complete three internships before they graduate. The Madeira schedule is set to offer large blocks of time for the girls to get real world experience in the Washington, DC, area. In the tenth grade, students participate in group community service placements. In eleventh grade, the girls intern on Capitol Hill, in a congressional office, or in an advocacy organization, while twelfth graders design their own internship, which is oriented toward their careers, including areas like computer science, research, business, government, or theater and the arts.

At NMH students spend three hours per week at their "workjob," which supports the idea that "being part of a community means playing your part in making that community run."[6] Students' workjob placements could involve baking in the dining hall, giving admissions tours, cleaning classrooms, maintaining hiking trails, tutoring, or working on NMH's farm, which includes a greenhouse, sugar house, a cider house, and live animals. Thirty students per year work on the farm, caring for animals, harvesting vegetables, pressing apples for cider, or collecting and boiling sap for maple syrup. One of my clients attended NMH many years ago and was so inspired by his work caring for farm animals that he became a veterinarian.

Holderness students participate in a jobs program "in which they work alongside the staff to help care for the wellbeing of the school."[7] Students work outside with the grounds crew, in the kitchen, by giving tours, or by focusing on campus recycling and sustainability efforts. At Kent School, every student has a job, which usually starts in the kitchen with washing dishes or setting up for dinner. Later in their school careers, they can apply for jobs at the library, in admissions, in tutoring, or in other areas of the school.

Students at Millbrook are lucky enough to have their own zoo on campus. The Trevor Zoo has more than 180 exotic and indigenous animals, including eight endangered species. As part of the community service program at Millbrook, students can work at the zoo, caring for the animals and acting as stewards of the natural world.

At Proctor, students on the Forestry Research Crew learn about forestry management on the vast 2,500-acre campus. They hike to all corners of the Proctor forest and "establish a long-term dataset that will inform [their] forest management."[8] Students learn about tree identification, mapping, compass use, tree measurement, data collection, and invasive species identification and removal. Proctor also has a Woods Team, which is comprised of a group of students who meet after classes at the Woodlands Center, where "they hop in the back of a pickup truck for a bumpy ride over woodland trails to clear new trails, repair bridges, clean up logging sites and identify trees for selective cutting. They split logs for wood-burning furnaces in dormitories, and deliver that cordwood to those dorms. In March, their focus turns to tapping the school's 300-plus maple trees, gathering sap and—best of all—boiling the sap into maple syrup in the sugarhouse. The Woods Team is a hearty crowd who love working outdoors on diverse tasks related to forestry and silviculture."[9]

Students at boarding schools have opportunities for work, service, and learning that simply aren't available in a typical high school. If your child is curious about the world and is interested in getting involved and learning new things, boarding school may offer her the chance to develop a new passion or a new understanding of the world. Whether it is through an internship, work with animals or in nature, or a simple campus job, these experiences are building blocks for students to become more engaged and involved with the world around them.

9

Athletics at Boarding Schools

Everyone's an athlete at boarding school. There is a place on the team for a student who has never played a sport, who has been cut from his local high school or town travel teams, or who simply wants to try something new. A sport for everyone is one of the great value propositions of boarding school life since kids benefit from the teamwork, camaraderie, and physical development of interscholastic athletics. On the flip side, athletes who want to take their game to a higher level can find top-ranked programs that can help them reach their goal of playing in college and beyond. Boarding schools manage this by having multiple teams, allowing all levels of athletes to benefit from participating in high school sports.

FINDING A NEW SPORT

I encourage my clients to try a sport, even if they have never played one, and to be sure to play a fall sport so they are part of a team during the first few months on campus. It's a great way to feel like a part of the school community right from the start. Most boarding schools require participation in one or two seasons of a team sport or other athletic activity. This makes up for the lack of a physical education class, which is a requirement that boarding school students are happy not to have.

I worked with a student named Lucas, who had given up on sports in sixth grade after not making the travel baseball team. As a freshman at Dublin School, he joined the mountain biking team and fell in love with the sport. He enjoyed being outdoors on the trail, as well as racing and competing. Lucas also played Ultimate in the spring and was happy to have found these two sports that were not offered in his hometown.

Grace was a student from China who had never participated in a team sport. She joined the "thirds" field hockey team at St. Mark's School, which is the team below junior varsity. There were many other new players, and she had fun learning the game and bonding with her teammates. Grace returned to the thirds team sophomore year and was happy to make junior varsity in eleventh grade.

Finn enrolled as a reclassed junior at New Hampton School, where he hoped to improve his grades and study habits for college. He had felt disconnected from his public high school and wasn't involved in any activities. He loved watching college and pro football, so he decided to ask for a manager position on the football team at New Hampton. I was surprised to get an excited email from Finn during the first week of school: "I'm not the manager, I am *playing* football! I'm on the team!" Finn later reflected that his time on the New Hampton football team was the pivotal experience of his teen years, one which improved his self-esteem and motivated him to work hard academically.

Carson was a student from Phoenix who tried crew during his freshman year at Kent School. He was over six feet tall at only fourteen years old, and he took to rowing immediately, thriving on teamwork and the feeling of being out on the water. He benefited from Kent's world-class rowing instruction and quickly achieved success in the sport. Soon he was going to regattas in Europe, placing high in the rankings, and excelling in the sport he loved. He was recruited by all the Ivy League colleges, and he accepted an offer from Princeton University, where he rowed collegiately. Carson was thankful for his boarding school experience since he would not have had the opportunity to row had he stayed in Phoenix for high school.

Crew, squash, fencing, and skiing are sports that are played at the college level but are not common at public schools or in most communities. Boarding school may be a student's only chance to try these sports, and for players with some experience, it may be their best chance to develop their skills and reach the level needed to play in college. Many students get excited about the nontraditional sports offered at boarding school, such as snowboarding, cycling, kayak racing, equestrian, mountain biking, figure skating, rock climbing, and Ultimate. These sports give students the opportunity to try something new and to compete in a sport that interests them.

ELITE ATHLETES AT BOARDING SCHOOL

For students who dream of playing their sports in college, on a professional team, or in the Olympics, boarding school is often the first step toward reaching their goals. Prep schools have always been a hotbed of top ice hockey activity, and sports such as rowing and squash, common at boarding schools, offer a seemingly direct path to a college team. But even with sports like basketball, swimming, skiing, golf, and others, it's common to find boarding school grads leading the way on their college team or beyond.

Elite athletes are drawn to boarding schools for the advanced level of competition and the chance to develop their game. But for them, even more is at stake than a typical student choosing a school. Athletes have to consider not only whether the school is a good fit academically, socially, and financially but also whether the athletic program will help them to excel during the critical high school years. Prospective athletes look for programs that are strong, with good coaching, skilled teammates, and opportunities for growth and improvement. Some will look for a sports team that is not so strong that they won't get playing time. They want a coach who is dedicated and driven but also one who is kind and believes in the players. Athletes also have to consider the opportunities they are leaving behind, which could be a club team, a favorite coach, teammates, or other commitments.

Athletes may consider reclassing, since moving back a year may help in the college recruiting process. Elite athletes and college sports hopefuls must first consider whether boarding school is right for them and then evaluate which athletic program will help them excel.

Ryan had big goals for his future in ice hockey. He dreamed of playing in the National Hockey League (NHL) or for an Ivy League hockey team, and he felt that prep ice hockey was the best way to get there. Ryan lived in suburban Connecticut and played for one of the top club teams, often attending tournaments or showcases in Canada and Europe. He was a ninth grader at a suburban public school with a good hockey team, but he chose not to play for the school team. Ryan's mother explained that it conflicted with club hockey and his training and that there wasn't enough competition on the team to make it worth his while. I was skeptical about the idea that Ryan was "too good" for the public school team, but I also knew that the family had successfully navigated the prep hockey world in the past. Ryan's older brother was a senior hockey player at Andover who had then committed to play at Yale after a stint in junior hockey.

Hayden was in ninth grade and also hoped to play Ivy League hockey. He attended a private school in New Jersey, where he had all As and was at the top of his class. Hayden played junior varsity in his freshman year and felt that he had a good chance of making varsity in sophomore year. However, he believed that attending a prep school could help him improve his hockey skills and get ready for the next level. He started researching schools, contacting hockey coaches, and scheduling interviews. Hayden was pleased to get responses from most of the coaches he contacted, but there were several that never responded and a few whose responses seemed tepid. One evening Hayden participated in a Hotchkiss Zoom call for prospective athletes to learn about the programs. He was disappointed to see over one hundred students on the call, including two from his club hockey team. It made him think that getting accepted would be harder than he anticipated.

Ryan emailed ten coaches and was worried that his brother's attendance at Andover would make the other coaches less interested in him. "I think Andover is my first choice, but I want to look at the other schools too," he reasoned. "But what if those coaches think I will follow my brother to Andover and won't talk to me?" All of the coaches responded to Ryan, and he had many email exchanges with them. Ryan worked hard at school, earning all As except for one B, which he'd received in honors biology. He studied with a tutor for the SSAT test and worked his way to an eighty-second percentile score.

For Hayden, his prep hockey dreams came to an end when he and his parents went to a Choate varsity hockey game. What they saw on the ice looked more like a college or professional game than high school hockey. The players were big, tall, and older—many were eighteen or nineteen years old due to reclassing. The play was fast, skilled, and physical. "I don't fit in here," Hayden said to his parents. They had watched enough hockey over the years to realize that Hayden was correct, and he was not likely to make varsity. Hayden decided to withdraw his applications and continue to play club and high school ice hockey at his current school.

Ryan completed seven applications to boarding schools, and he emailed or spoke with all the coaches. Many of them watched him play at his club tournaments in the fall, and he spoke to a few of them in person after his interviews. When the decisions came out in March, Ryan was accepted to five of the schools he'd applied to and was wait-listed at two. He decided to follow his brother's lead to Andover.

ATHLETES IN THE ADMISSIONS PROCESS

The most common way to start the recruiting process for boarding school sports is to complete the recruited athlete form on the school's website or to email the coach of your sport directly. This introduction of your student athlete can open up the conversation, allowing the coach to learn about her experience and skills while also helping you to learn more about the school and sports team. It's not only the elite athletes who complete these forms but also any athlete with some experience who plans to participate in the sport in high school. It's not a required step to playing a sport in boarding school, but it offers a chance for strong athletes to make themselves known to the coaches, which could help them in the admissions process.

At Berkshire School they receive about four hundred inquiry forms for boys' ice hockey each year. The Williston Northampton girls' ice hockey team receives about 150–175 inquiry forms, which leads to approximately ninety applications. Other schools report about one hundred inquiries for lacrosse, basketball, soccer, and other popular sports. Hundreds of students start the recruiting process, but by the end, only about four to eight new students for each sport will be enrolling each fall. That doesn't mean there will be only four to eight new lacrosse players or new ice hockey players, since there will be many more new students playing those sports each year. But it's this small number of students who will get preferential treatment in the admissions process.

In addition to the inquiry forms, some coaches find prospective athletes at club team tournaments or at showcases, such as the Pre-Prep and Pathways to Prep Showcases for ice hockey. There are a few state athletic associations that don't allow recruiting of any kind, such as those in Michigan and Florida, which means that schools such as Cranbrook and Bolles field teams without any formal recruiting process. Athletes who reach out to coaches in these states are first referred to the admissions office.

Once the coaches have a list of interested athletes, it's time to evaluate them. Coaches review the applicant's sports resume, watch film, and email or talk with the student by phone or Zoom, then meet them in person when they come to campus. Kevin Czepiel, head coach of the Berkshire School boys' varsity hockey team, says that he likes to see prospects play hockey live, and he travels around the Northeast in the fall, watching their games. He looks for strong players but also students with high grades and other interests. Czepiel only rarely talks to an applicant's coach for a club or prior school, partly because his own evaluation is thorough enough but because many prospective players don't want their current coach to know they are considering leaving the team.

At Lawrenceville, home of the number one boys' lacrosse team in the country, head coach Jon Posner receives about 250 inquiry forms per year. But most of the eight candidates he ultimately brings to the admissions committee are players he discovered at club lacrosse tournaments. He spends the summer attending club lacrosse tournaments, taking notes, and contacting parents of the players who stand out. As for the inquiry forms, Posner said, "Sometimes we get lucky and find a player and will go look at him," noting that he watches all of his players on the field before recruiting them.[1]

When Posner evaluates a player, he looks for "talent and skill level. Speed is first. Stick skills are important. But what I really look at is how hard they play out there." After identifying them on the field, Posner looks at their character, which he assesses through conversations with the boys' parents, coaches, and with the players themselves. And because Lawrenceville has a rigorous academic program, Posner has to be sure that the student can do the work, thrive, and excel academically. Once he decides the student is a good fit for Lawrenceville and the lacrosse program, he makes the family know that the boy is wanted. This includes conversations, letters sent to the player in the mail, and emails. This helps the family to learn more about Lawrenceville and the lacrosse program while they are going through the admissions process. Posner brings about eight prospective players to the admissions committee each year. His hard work in recruiting has brought him a 100 percent yield, meaning all of the students he has brought to committee during his three years at Lawrenceville have accepted the offer and enrolled.

In sports like swimming, track, and rowing, coaches can look at performance times as an evaluation factor. Peter Verhoef, head swim coach at Bolles School, shares, "With swimming being an objective sport, we start with top performances. When I look up a swimmer's times I'm looking at the range of events they can swim—we like to see between five and seven different events, their improvement rate year over year, consistency of competition (do they compete year-round), and what meets their current performances qualify them for."[2]

Coaches prefer to communicate with the applicant rather than the parents, but they do understand that for younger applicants, many of whom are only thirteen years old, it can be awkward to talk with a coach they have never met before and parental help may be needed. Christa Talbot-Syfu, head coach of the Williston Northampton School girls' ice hockey team, prefers to communicate with players through email, and she responds to every student who contacts her. Applicants contact coaches during the fall of their application year, and some continue email contact through the winter.

When it's time for the admissions committee to meet in January and February of the application year, coaches bring their list of preferred students forward. These students are then screened for academic fit, as the committees trust that the list represents players the coach feels would contribute to the team and the school as a whole. Christa Talbot-Syfu makes sure her selected applicants "are players who will make an impact," saying, "I like to make sure they are a good fit for Williston, and I like to see them play other sports too."[3] Of her initial 150–175 hockey inquiries, about 90 will apply, and she will support about ten applicants in admissions, knowing that they won't all attend Williston.

Contrary to popular belief, there are no athletic scholarships in boarding school. While athletes are eligible for need-based aid like any other students, there are no scholarships awarded for athletic talent at the traditional boarding schools. I frequently have parents tell me that they heard about someone who received a sports scholarship to boarding school. But although the student may have connected with the coach and received preferential treatment in admissions, he didn't receive a scholarship to play that sport. He most likely received need-based financial aid, with the amount determined by his parent's income and assets, or a merit scholarship based on overall academic and extracurricular excellence.

THINGS TO CONSIDER WHEN EVALUATING ATHLETIC PROGRAMS

Parents of serious athletes can speak with coaches and get a sense of the program philosophy and competitiveness of the league. They should consider the path for progression since their athlete may be starting on a junior varsity team and moving up during their years at the school. It can be hard to judge how your student will do over the years, particularly at schools who bring in new upperclassmen or post graduate students.

Schools that offer a postgraduate year for students who have completed high school, often called PGs, may have eighteen- and nineteen-year-old players coming in for one year, which can impact the playing time of younger students. Most leagues limit the number of PGs allowed in each sport so there won't be an overwhelming number of older players. But for a sophomore who hopes to get varsity playing time, he may find that the presence of reclassed juniors and PG students will make that difficult. On the other hand, exceptional athletes welcome the chance to compete at the highest level, and it's common for strong sophomores and juniors to compete and play on varsity, even with the reclassed and PG students.

Some athletes are drawn to schools that don't allow PG students so that they may have a better chance at making varsity or getting the playing time they want. The Independent School League, or ISL, in New England does not allow PG students and includes schools such as Brooks, Governor's, Groton, Lawrence, Middlesex, Milton, St. George's, St. Mark's, and Tabor. George and Westtown are in a Pennsylvania league that doesn't allow PGs, as are Episcopal, Georgetown Prep, and many schools outside of the Northeast, where PG programs are most commonly found. Cranbrook, located in Michigan, whose state athletic association restricts recruiting and doesn't allow PGs or reclass students, is able to field a competitive national-level hockey team. Parents who are looking for schools with typical-age high school students may want to consider adding schools without PG students to their list.

However, it's important to note that PGs and reclassed athletes are not a factor in all sports, so this isn't something that all parents of athletes should be evaluating. Sports such as ice hockey, boys' basketball, and football have the largest number of PGs and reclassed students. Girls' sports have fewer PG and reclassed students than boys' sports teams.

OVERVIEW OF SELECTED BOARDING SCHOOL SPORTS PROGRAMS

Basketball

Boarding schools with elite boys' basketball programs offer both a typical high school team as well as a "national" team, which consists of top players from around the world who have dreams of playing Division 1 college or NBA basketball. The average basketball player can go to any boarding school and find a junior varsity to varsity pathway with the opportunity to play and improve. At basketball powerhouses, they also offer one or more higher level teams that play a competitive schedule and pack the gyms with college coaches.

Brewster Academy has a boys' national team that competes in the Nike Elite Youth Basketball League and has a busy schedule, with thirty games and tournaments across the United States, many of which are televised by ESPN. Brewster also has a boys' prep team that competes in AAA, the highest division of the New England Preparatory School Athletic Council (NEPSAC), and a boys' varsity team, which competes in the B division of NEPSAC and is run like a typical high school program. There are also two boys' junior varsity teams and a girls' varsity and junior varsity team. Over 170 Brewster alumni have played Division 1 basketball, and 21 have played in the NBA.

Montverde Academy, eight-time High School National Basketball Championship winner, had a 33–0 season in 2024 and recently finished at the top of ESPN's ranking of high school basketball teams. Montverde offers a national team and a program called the Center for Basketball Development, which includes three varsity and three junior varsity teams for boys.

Oak Hill Academy, which routinely sends players to college and professional basketball, offers a gold team, for upper Division 1 level talent, as well as red and white teams for players who also aspire to play basketball in college. Oak Hill's international team is for players from abroad to get an introduction to the American style of play.

Hargrave has a consistently strong basketball program that draws college coaches to their games and practices. In the recent March Madness college basketball championships, there were thirteen Hargrave graduates either playing or coaching in the tournament, and nineteen of their alumni have played in the NBA.

Scholar athletes look to Northfield Mt. Hermon's basketball program since they are the leader in Ivy League commitments. In the last fifteen years, forty-five NMH students have graduated to Ivy League basketball, which is three times the number of any other high school. NMH plays in the top NEPSAC conference and offers a strong academic and basketball combination.

In girls' basketball, Blair Academy leads the field with recent state titles, a McDonald's All-American, and ten recent graduates playing at the Division 1 level. The boys' team at Blair is also a basketball powerhouse, with over eighty graduates playing at the college level, twelve playing professionally internationally, five in the NBA, and one coaching an NBA team.

Equestrian

Horse lovers and experienced equestrians can find opportunities for competition, fun, and time with horses and other horse lovers at boarding schools. Some schools have a barn on campus, and a student can even bring her own horse. Students can compete with other schools, participate in rated and unrated shows, or simply learn about horses and horsemanship. Some schools travel to a barn off campus and offer everything from beginner lessons to advanced competition. Thacher School has a horse program that is an essential part of the school culture. All ninth graders are paired with a horse during the first week of school and required to ride and learn about horsemanship. Every student goes on a weekend horse packing trip, and some choose to participate in the Big Gymkhana, which is a western-style equestrian competition.

The girls' schools have led the way in equestrian programs, with the following schools offering programs: Chatham Hall, Dana Hall, Ethel Walker, Foxcroft, Garrison Forest, Grier, Linden Hall, Madeira, Miss Hall's, Miss Porter's, Stoneleigh Burnham, and St. Timothy's. Coed schools with equestrian opportunities include Asheville, Canterbury, Christchurch, Culver, Fountain Valley, George, Gould, Kent, Kimball Union, Knox, Loomis Chaffee, Marvelwood, Proctor, Putney, and Thacher, among others.

Football

Football, with its rivalries, tailgating, and homecoming games, is a fun part of boarding school life. At most schools, anyone can join the football team since experience isn't required, only an interest in the game and a willingness to work hard at it. Not all boarding schools have football, since many are too small to field a team, while some larger schools, such as NMH, have ended their football programs. Top football boarding schools include Choate, which, in the last seven years, has had eighty-eight alumni play football in college and two play in the NFL; Cheshire, with over one hundred graduates in college football; and Baylor, which recently had a state championship football team with five seniors committed to play at top Division 1 football programs, plus four NFL alumni. Fork Union has had more than one hundred graduates play in the NFL, including several Heisman Trophy winners. They have a competitive varsity program, as well as a PG football team that competes against college teams. Other top boarding school football programs include Exeter, Hun, Deerfield, and Avon Old Farms. Boarding schools listed among the Top 100 high school football programs as ranked by the NFL include McCallie, Rabun Gap-Nacoochee, Baylor, and IMG.

Golf

The weather and the length of the competitive season are important considerations for aspiring golfers. At schools in New England that have a spring golf season, the weather can be cold and wet in March and April, causing cancellations and a shorter playing schedule. Despite the weather, many New England schools have vibrant golf programs, which often include indoor simulators or winter trips to Florida to train or compete. New England schools that have a fall golf season allowing for more playing time include Brewster, Kents Hill, Hebron, and Gould. The mild weather in California and the Southern states allows for more days of golf, which draws the avid golfer. Schools with notable golf programs in warmer areas include Darlington, St. Stephen's, McCallie, and St. Andrew's of Florida. Facilities may be a consideration, but most schools without golf courses have made arrangements for their teams to practice at local courses. For Stevenson School in Pebble Beach, California, this means matches and practices at world-class courses in their area. Hotchkiss and Peddie have their own golf courses.

There is a golf dynasty at Baylor, where the boys' and girls' golf teams have won forty state championships plus twenty-one individual championships, and the school has had alumni play in six of the last ten Master's tournaments. There are currently four Professional Golfers' Association (PGA) and one Ladies' Professional Golfers' Association (LPGA) players who are graduates of Baylor.

Shattuck-St. Mary's School has a "Golf Center of Excellence," which combines a college prep academic program with a full school year of golf, including a tour style schedule that includes several trips to Florida.[4] Students can play on the school's eighteen-hole golf course or practice in their 2,800 square foot indoor facility that has heated practice bays and chipping and putting courses.

Aspiring golfers who want an intensive golf experience consider golf academies, which are primarily located in Florida and South Carolina. These schools, including IMG, Junior Players Golf Academy, International Junior Golf Academy, and Golf Performance Academy, have top instruction and golf opportunities in a less traditional academic setting.

Ice Hockey

The highest level of youth ice hockey is played in the Minnesota, Michigan, and New England prep schools. Students who want to learn hockey or reach new heights in their own game will find top coaching and facilities in boarding school, particularly in New England.

In boys' ice hockey, Cushing has been a perennial top-ranked program, having produced eighteen NHL players and five Olympians. Kimball Union, another hockey powerhouse, defeated Cushing this year to win the coveted NEPSAC championship. There are sixty-four teams in New England prep hockey, with the Elite Eight making it to the playoffs. Hockey players attending any of these schools will get a strong hockey education and the chance to take their game as far as it will go. Schools with strong hockey programs include Salisbury; Avon Old Farms, which has four teams (including varsity and varsity B); and Frederick Gunn, which has a small-school experience with top-level hockey. At South Kent School, the hockey program is over one hundred years old and has produced more than one hundred Division 1 college players and twenty-four NHL players. Their program is unique since players compete in AAA club hockey based on age rather than competing in traditional scholastic hockey.

Williston Northampton, coached for twenty-one years by Christa Talbot-Syfu, is a dominant force in girls' hockey. The team has been the top boarding school in the NEPSAC conference over the recent years, and graduates are playing college hockey at Harvard, Brown, and Amherst. Other top girls' hockey programs include Andover, Loomis Chaffee, Kent, Choate, Deerfield, Tabor, St. Paul's, and Groton. Ivy League and New England Small College Athletic Association (NESCAC) team rosters are filled with girls' ice hockey players from these schools.

At Berkshire School there are two rinks, which provides plenty of ice time for the boys' and girls' teams. Czepiel says, "We have three teams for boys and three for girls, so there is room for kids to develop and move up."[5] At most boarding schools, the hockey players play with local club teams during weekends in the fall. At Williston Northampton the hockey players on the girls' team get ice time twice a week in the off-season, plus they often play for local club teams. The NEPSAC girls' coaches have recently started to collaborate with club teams and host three showcases each fall, which is an important part of college recruiting.

Shattuck St. Mary's School offers the Hockey Center of Excellence, which is a rigorous seven-month intensive hockey program paired with a full college prep curriculum. Open to both boys and girls, the teams play fifty to sixty games a year and travel throughout the United States and Canada. Students have ice time six to seven days a week and participate in conditioning and preparation for their future in hockey. Shattuck St. Mary's has a long track record of success in hockey with 32 USA hockey national championships, 103 NHL draft picks, 21 Olympians, and over 700 collegiate hockey players.

Lacrosse

The first documented high school lacrosse games were held at Andover, Exeter, and Lawrenceville in 1882. There was so little competition back then that these schools played against college teams. Today the sport of lacrosse is booming, and boys' and girls' lacrosse teams are found at the majority of boarding schools in the United States.

The nation's top high school lacrosse teams have historically been concentrated at public and private schools located in the lacrosse hotbed areas of the country, such as Maryland, Long Island, and upstate New York. But recently, boys' prep lacrosse has emerged as a leader in the lacrosse world.

Culver and Lawrenceville are two boarding schools that made the list of the USA Lacrosse Top 20 teams recently, and both were led by coach Jon Posner. Culver reached number one in the Inside Lacrosse rankings in 2019 and won the National Prep Championship, the top tournament for private schools. Posner joined Lawrenceville in 2020 and brought his penchant for recruiting and molding championship teams to the New Jersey school. One of Posner's secrets to success is simple: practice. The Lawrenceville lacrosse team works and trains hard, focusing on improving individual and team weaknesses. In 2024 Lawrenceville was unanimously named the number one high school team in the country by Inside Lacrosse, the National Lacrosse Federation, and by USA Lacrosse. This Lawrenceville championship team included twenty-seven juniors and seniors who committed to play Division 1 college lacrosse.

In girls' lacrosse Hotchkiss is the only boarding school to crack the USA Lacrosse Top 20 list. Coached by Britt Giacco, Hotchkiss has a winning tradition that includes more than ten Founders League Championships since 2015. The team recently traveled to New Zealand to play internationally and enjoy a team-bonding experience. Hotchkiss lacrosse graduates are bringing their talents to college, playing at Dartmouth, Princeton, Brown, Penn, University of North Carolina Chapel Hill (UNC), and others.

Rowing

There are more than sixty boarding schools that offer rowing. It's common to join a rowing team with no experience at all, and it's one of the few sports where athletes don't have to feel behind if they didn't start the sport at a young age. In fact, most rowing clubs don't start until middle school, and some crew coaches suggest waiting until at least eighth grade to start this sport.

Kent has one of the leading high school rowing programs, with over one hundred years of history on the Housatonic River. The program focuses on character development and teamwork, and it brings its rowers to regattas around the country. The school has a boathouse and an indoor rowing tank, offering year-round rowing opportunities for boys and girls. Deerfield, Exeter, and St. Paul's also have notable rowing programs.

Sailing

Experienced sailors are drawn to school programs where they can compete in regattas and vie for the Baker Cup, which is the national championship of the Interscholastic Sailing Association (ISSA). Most boarding school sailing teams are coed, have about forty to fifty sailors, and comprise a mix of experienced and new participants. Schools with sailing programs include Christchurch, Hotchkiss, Milton, Portsmouth Abbey, St. George's, Stony Brook, Tabor, and Taft, among others.

Outside of competitive sailing, Tabor and St. George's offer programs that introduce students to marine science, nautical science, and seamanship. Tabor has the SSV *Tabor Boy*, a 115-foot, two-masted schooner used for one-week summer cruises for new students as well as research and training. At St. George's, the *Geronimo* is a seventy-foot cutter used for educational sailing excursions. The eight-student crew participates in all aspects of sailing the *Geronimo* on trips that last from one to six weeks in length and often include transatlantic voyages.

Skiing

For boarding schools located near the mountains of New England, skiing is a big part of the school culture. Often, classes end early during ski season, and more than half the students spend their afternoons on the snow. Boarding schools offer programs in alpine ski racing, Nordic skiing, freeskiing, freestyle, ski jumping, and snowboarding. Some programs are intensive, with many hours of training and a focus on technical skills, which are cultivated by gate training and work with airbags, as well as trips abroad to ski in the off-season. Schools can compete in the NEPSAC league or, for more serious athletes, the US Ski and Snowboard Association races. Aspiring skiers should evaluate the programs carefully to find a good fit.

Proctor Academy has its own ski area, including a mountain with lighted trails, snowmaking, and a ski jump. They have high-level training for Olympic hopefuls, as well as lessons for beginners. Experienced skiers can even participate in ski patrol as an afterschool activity. Eaglebrook, a junior boarding school, also has its own ski area with snowmaking and a chair lift, as does Kents Hill School. Other boarding schools with strong ski programs include Gould, Northwood, Holderness, Brewster, Kents Hill, Kimball Union, and Northfield Mt. Hermon, among others.

"Ski academies" have been around for many years and have produced scores of Olympians and collegiate skiers. These small boarding schools have intensive ski training programs that are paired with college prep academics. East Coast schools include Burke Mountain Academy, which has had thirty-nine Olympians; Carrabassett Valley Academy; Green Mountain Valley School; Killington Mountain School; and Stratton Mountain School. In the West, top ski academies include Lake Tahoe Prep, Rowmark Ski Academy, Sugar Bowl Academy, Steamboat Mountain School, Sun Valley Ski Academy, and Wy'East Mountain Academy.

Soccer

Soccer is a unifying sport at boarding school since so many students from around the world have played the sport at some point in their lives. New students often try soccer since it is a fall sport and it offers the chance to be a part of a school team during those first few months at school.

South Kent has a leading boys' soccer program, with six national championships and seventy-five graduates playing on Division 1 soccer teams. Berkshire is a leader in the NEPSAC league, and in addition to having a strong on-campus training program, the team occasionally travels internationally for tournaments. McCallie has a top program in the South, playing an aggressive out-of-state schedule and sending seven athletes to Division 1 soccer over a recent five-year period. St. Stephen's offers a soccer academy, which is an intensive training program that lasts the entire school year. Pennington has a strong tradition in boys' soccer, drawing student athletes from all over the world.

Pennington is also a leader in girls' soccer, with a top national ranking and a strong schedule. The team has reached the state finals almost every year since the 1980s and won the title in all but four appearances. Sixteen recent Pennington girls' soccer alumni were captains on their college teams. Baylor girls' soccer program was ranked number two in the nation by MaxPreps and won the Tennessee State championship in 2023.

Players interested in an intensive soccer program can consider IMG Academy or the Shattuck St. Mary's Soccer Center for Excellence.

Squash

Squash is known as an individual sport, but in the boarding school world, there is plenty of camaraderie around team squash. New players, particularly those who have played tennis or other racquet sports, can get on the court and successfully play squash fairly quickly. Those who are serious about the sport play on the school squash team as a way to supplement the training they do outside of school. Most play US Squash Association tournaments for a ranking outside of school.

Each winter, the US Squash Association hosts the US High School Squash Championships in Philadelphia. It's the largest squash tournament in the world, with 1,600 players coming from two hundred different schools, many of them boarding schools. Schools with top squash programs for boys and girls include Andover, Deerfield, Hill, Hotchkiss, Kent, Lawrenceville, Milton, St. Andrew's of Florida, St. Paul's, Tabor, and Taft.

Swimming

Most boarding school swim teams are open to anyone who wants to participate, but there are a few top national programs that draw those who dream of swimming in college or the Olympics. Bolles School is synonymous with swimming success, and they have had alumni in every Olympics since 1972, with a total of sixty-three Olympians, including fourteen gold medal winners. Bolles is perennially at the top of the rankings of *Swimming World* and offers a year-round program with excellent coaching. The Bolles swim program has twenty to twenty-five new students each year, who come from more than ten different countries. Bolles operates a USA Swimming club team, so the swimmers have continuity between school and club swimming, and the school is able to provide year-round training and competitions. Bolles has two pools: an Olympic sized fifty-meter pool and a smaller competition pool. Other schools with top swim programs include Baylor, Peddie, and St. Andrew's of Florida.

Tennis

Many lifelong tennis players got their start at boarding school. Whether they are playing doubles or singles on the varsity team or recreationally, boarding school students have fun with tennis and improve their skills each year. Students who want to play tennis in college work toward improving their Universal Tennis Rating, or UTR, by training and playing matches.

Many athletes look toward tennis academies, which offer a competitive atmosphere and an intensive regimen along with the academic work done online or in-person during part of the school day. Legendary tennis coach Nick Bollettieri pioneered the idea of a tennis boarding school when he established the Nick Bollettieri Tennis Academy in the 1980s. World-class players such as Andre Agassi and Monica Seles famously trained at the academy, which led to greater acceptance of the model where children and teens train away from home; this model sparked the establishment of other tennis boarding schools. The Nick Bollettieri Academy was sold to IMG, now the leader in tennis training. Other tennis academies include Weil, Everet, Van Der Meer, and Saddlebrook.

St. Stephen's Episcopal School offers a tennis academy that combines the traditional college prep boarding program with intensive tennis training. Students attend a full day of classes and are part of the St. Stephen's boarding community. After school they go to a fourteen-court facility, where a team of pros works individually with players, arranges matches, and conducts group training and conditioning work.

10

✢

The Arts at Boarding Schools

The arts are celebrated at boarding schools. Young artists can enjoy state-of-the-art facilities, a wide array of courses, dedicated teachers, and a like-minded peer group. Whether your student plans to dabble in art, try something new, or create a portfolio for college or art school admission, he will find that many schools have an art program to support his interests. Every school offers a visual arts program, and most have theater productions, so students in those areas will find a variety of options. Music programs vary, with some schools offering only choral and others offering both choral and instrumental or even string music programs. Dance is not offered at every school, but those that do offer it often have programs that send students to the advanced dance company level. Families who are interested in visual arts, music, theater, or dance should evaluate programs at schools of interest by looking at the course and extracurricular offerings, then digging in for deeper research by speaking with students and faculty about their offerings and experience in the arts.

Admissions committees are looking for artists, so if your student can dance, sing, paint, or contribute to the arts community, it's important to show that in the application. The SAO (https://www.admission.org/services/standard-application-online-sao) and Gateway (https://www.gatewaytoprepschools.com/) applications have a multimedia section where applicants can upload their art work. This can be a video of a student's violin performance, scenes from a play, or a video or slide show featuring a drawing, painting, or sculpture. Anything creative or artistic can be highlighted in the multimedia section of the application. Students who already submitted their application but later realized they want to share something artistic with the admissions team can simply email a link to their interviewer.

During the application process, applicants can reach out to boarding school arts teachers through email and arrange a Zoom call or a personal meeting during an on-campus visit. This personal connection with a staff member in the arts department helps the student learn more about the program but also gives the school representatives the chance to get to know the applicant. When the admissions committee meets, the art department heads bring forward the applicants they feel will make an immediate contribution to school life. This "recruiting," or preferences in admissions for accomplished artists, can help an applicant stand out in the admissions process.

VISUAL ARTS

Cranbrook School offers a vast art program that includes sculpting, weaving, and metalsmithing, all with experienced teachers in each discipline. Artists in the weaver and fiber arts area work on collage, tapestry, sewing, embroidery, and computerized weaving. Metalsmith students use copper, brass, and bronze, and their instruction comprises forging, soldering, and construction of three-dimensional forms, including jewelry. The Cranbrook campus is architecturally significant and includes an art deco home and a Frank Lloyd Wright house. An art museum on campus has two hundred thousand visitors annually and includes over six thousand pieces of art and a sculpture garden.

Cushing Academy has a strong arts program with many Scholastic Art Award winners, as well as a popular visual arts magazine that showcases student work. The Cushing arts facility includes studios for pottery and sculpture, photography, metalsmithing, and glass. Artists working with glass learn to solder, cut glass, paint on glass, and make glass jewelry, among other things. Cushing students can also study architectural design.

Masters School has a studio art major program and a school philosophy of portfolio development for each student. Classes are offered in architecture, design, crafts, filmmaking, game design, animation, motion graphics, and many other areas. Other schools that offer strong art programs and campus communities that celebrate the arts include Besant Hill, Buxton, Miss Hall's, and Putney, among others. Salisbury School offers arts programs in wood shop and has a boat-building studio where students make sea kayaks and small wooden boats.

MUSIC

Most boarding schools offer choral programs that may include ensembles, a large chorus, or private lessons and voice study. Students who want to play instrumental music should research schools, as some of them have small—or no—instrumental offerings, while others offer vibrant programs with lots of participation.

Choate has many musicians, and the school offers opportunities for them to practice, perform, and study music. It also has a symphony orchestra, concert orchestra, wind ensemble, jazz combo group, chamber chorus, festival chorus, a cappella groups, plus a variety of student-directed groups and opportunities to jam. They have many concerts and recitals each term. Concord Academy offers classes in music theory, composition, and recording technology. Other schools with strong music programs include Andover, Blair, Deerfield, Exeter, Hotchkiss, Lawrenceville, Loomis Chaffee, and Milton, among others.

DANCE

The preeminent boarding school dance program is at St. Paul's School, where dancers of all levels can participate in classes and learn from top professional teachers. The school hosts an audition-only dance company with a world-class reputation that has prepared students for college and professional careers in their fields. St. Paul's website describes their esteemed program:

> Serious dancers may audition for the St. Paul's School Ballet Company (SPSBC), a year-round program that can be substituted for athletic participation at the varsity level. SPSBC dancers work one-on-one with faculty and guest teachers and choreographers, rehearsing daily throughout the academic calendar, and performing four different programs per school year. Its repertory includes classics as well as contemporary works. Guest teachers and choreographers have included members of internationally recognized companies such as American Ballet Theatre, Dance Theatre of Harlem, BalletX, The Balanchine Trust, Mikhail Baryshnikov's White Oak Dance Project, Merce Cunningham Dance Company, Twyla Tharp, New York City Ballet, Paul Taylor Dance Company and Batsheva Dance Company.[1]

At Grier School, more than half the student body studies dance each year. Serious dancers can participate in Grier's Pre-Professional Dance Program, which includes thirty hours of instruction a week. Girls in the program take classes only in the morning and then spend the afternoon, from 12:30 to 6:30 p.m., in the dance studio, taking ballet, modern, jazz, and contemporary dance classes.

Parents of dancers should evaluate the dance programs at boarding schools of interest. The mother of a girl who chose

Miss Porter's for its combination of academics and dance commented, "We looked at schools with dedicated dance companies and traditional afterschool programs. My daughter auditioned at St. Paul's, but it didn't feel like the right level for her. We attended a dance preview session at Miss Porter's, and she had the chance to dance and participate. She liked the teachers and the girls, and everything about it just felt right."

When you visit campus, it's important to speak with current dancers and dance teachers. Sometimes you can observe a class—or even participate in one. Questions that are commonly asked about boarding school dance programs include the following:

- Do you have a dance company with an audition process?
- What options are there for dancers who don't make the dance company?
- What is the focus of your dance program (ballet, modern, etc.)?
- How many hours a day do your dancers have practice?
- Does dance count as an athletic requirement?

Dedicated dancers often consider these schools: Andover, Choate, Deerfield, Emma Willard, Ethel Walker, Grier, Mercersburg, Milton, Miss Porter's, and St. Paul's, among many others.

THEATER

Most boarding schools offer a theater program of some kind, but this can range from one casual production per year at some schools to others that offer an intensive drama program with multiple large and small productions, theatrical troupes, and academic study of the dramatic arts. Students evaluating theater programs often consider the number of productions offered per year, the facilities, the drama courses, and the overall participation and vibrance of the theater department.

Prospective actors can research online, email theater program directors, meet with them during on-campus visits, or attend a production, all of which are good ways to determine the fit of the theater offerings.

St. Stephen's Episcopal School offers the Theater Focus program, which creates a sense of community and belonging for students while also helping them develop their craft. Students attend master classes, work with visiting instructors, attend private lessons, travel to theater performances in the region, and practice and prepare for their own performances. The program also helps students prepare for outside auditions and with the college application process for future theater majors.

Dominic Sessa was a Deerfield Academy student who found his way to a starring role in a Hollywood movie through his school theater department. He was cast as Angus in *The Holdovers*, for which he received the 2024 Critics Choice Award for Best Young Actor.[2] Sessa was active in the theater program at Deerfield, taking acting and directing classes, and he performed in plays, such as *Antigone.*

In an article in the *Deerfield Scroll*, Sessa explained that "Deerfield theater classes are small . . . you feel a sort of conservatory type of an atmosphere, where you create these ensembles." He elaborated, "You really are able to make more in-depth relationships that you maybe wouldn't be able to make in any other classes because you're on your feet and are pushed to be very vulnerable. You have to show sides of yourself that you may not be very motivated to show in other areas on campus."[3]

The directors of the film *The Holdovers* contacted several boarding school theater directors to conduct auditions for the role of Angus. Twelve Deerfield students auditioned, and Dominic Sessa was awarded the role that launched his acting career.

ARTS-FOCUSED BOARDING SCHOOLS

Students who want the arts to be a core part of their day rather than an afterschool activity consider arts-specialty boarding schools. At these three arts-centered boarding schools, there is a traditional academic component, but there are also about four hours a day of arts instruction or practice. Students enjoy an arts-focused campus culture, along with an artistic peer group and lots of enthusiasm for campus arts events.

Interlochen Art Academy in Interlochen, Michigan, has over five hundred students living and learning in a community of artists. According to the school website, "the Interlochen experience is a vibrant journey of creativity and camaraderie."[4] Students can focus in the following areas: dance, film and new media, interdisciplinary arts, music, theater, or visual arts. The students benefit from a guest artist program, and it's on the site of the world-famous Interlochen Arts Camp, which hosts three thousand students from all over the world.

Idyllwild Arts Academy in Idyllwild, California, is a vibrant community with 50 percent of its students coming from thirty different countries. Idyllwild offers art majors, which include dance, fashion design, film and digital media, interarts, music, dramatic arts, and visual arts.

Walnut Hill School for the Arts in Natick, Massachusetts, has 290 students, one-third of whom are international students. The areas of focus include dance, music, theater, visual arts, writing, film, and media arts.

11

International Students at Boarding Schools

Parents are often surprised at the number of international students at boarding schools and at the diversity of the countries they come from. International students make up more than half the population at some schools and as few as 5 percent at others. Andover and Choate have student populations comprising 15 percent and 18 percent international students, respectively, a typical percentage among the selective boarding schools. Students come from thirty or forty different countries, and many schools display the flag of each student's home country in the dining hall or another space at the school.

There are currently about seventy thousand international high school students studying in the US.[1] These students are on F1 or J1 visas and attend boarding schools or day schools (while in the care of host families), or they enroll in exchange programs at private or public schools. With such a large number of high school students seeking to study in the United States, many day schools have opened up dorms or homestay programs to accommodate international students. It's a huge market for boarding schools, day schools, and Catholic schools throughout the United States. It's important for parents considering a high school education in the United States to weigh all the options, as there can be vast differences in quality and in price.

I'm impressed with the students who leave their home country for educational opportunities, and I also admire the parents who sacrifice to let them go. International students face a challenging application process and higher tuition fees, often with limited options for financial aid. Once they arrive in the United States, they have to adapt to American teen culture, combat homesickness, and excel in an unfamiliar academic environment, often in a new language. It's a lot to ask of a student who is just out of middle school. Let's examine the world of boarding schools for those coming from outside the United States.

INTERNATIONAL STUDENT ADMISSIONS PROCESS

There are a few added steps and complications for international students in the boarding school admissions process. They may have to contend with a language barrier and time change difficulties when scheduling meetings or connecting with schools. Some schools have made their website available in multiple languages, and many use online scheduling or email, which can make connecting across time zones easier. Interviews are often during the school day in the host school's time zone, but several boarding schools have added late afternoon and evening interview time slots that add flexibility.

Vericant (www.vericant.com) is a third-party interview service that is used to assess the English language skills of applicants from non-English speaking countries. At some schools, Vericant is required for all applicants from China, and at others, it is used selectively, so be sure to check the admissions web page of each school you are applying to. The Vericant interviews take place in studios in Beijing, Shanghai, and Shenzhen, and they are conducted electronically for applicants from other areas. The Vericant interview is designed to test spoken English skills, but the admissions staff watching the interviews also get a sense of what the student is like and how she can contribute to the school community, just as they would if they were conducting the interview themselves. Students are asked to describe a photograph, and they are given in-depth questions, such as being asked to talk about a challenge they have overcome in the past or their hopes and dreams for studying abroad. After the spoken interview, students take a proctored writing test, where they complete a short essay.

An English language test, such as the Test of English as a Foreign Language (TOEFL iBT), the International English Language Testing System (IELTS), or Duolingo, is required for students who live in a non-English speaking country and attend a school whose language of instruction is not English. The testing requirement is typically waived for students who have studied for at least three years in a school with English as its primary language of instruction. Selective boarding schools require fluency in English, and the guideline for these schools is a score of 100 on the TOEFL, 7.5 on the IELTS, or 125 on Duolingo. Those scores represent fluency and comfort with the casual, spoken English language. Students who are not fluent should consider schools that offer English language learner classes and have a lower testing requirement for entry.

Students with transcripts in languages other than English must arrange to have them translated. They also have to arrange for teacher recommendations and school counselor reports to be sent in English. At many schools abroad, they don't have a school counselor, and staff members are unfamiliar with writing recommendations, so parents may have to help the school staff through this part of the process. It's best to start early and leave extra time for getting transcripts and letters of recommendation translated and submitted.

Chapter 11

SELECTIVE SCHOOLS AND INTERNATIONAL ADMISSIONS

Rasul was a fourteen-year-old boy from Kazakhstan who was determined to come to America to attend a well-known high school. He also planned to attend an elite university, then achieve financial and career success in the United States. It was a hefty dream for a young teen, one which actually came from his parents and extended family. They spoke about their dreams for Rasul often, instilling in him the desire to take risks, to achieve, and to look for opportunities.

When I started working with Rasul, he was attending the equivalent of the eighth grade at a boarding school in England. This was intended to be the first stop on his journey to America, a time for him to become fluent in English and get used to Western culture. In my meetings with Rasul's family, it was Rasul who served as our translator, as neither of his parents spoke English. Throughout our year working together, Rasul translated all of our meetings, plus the emails that I sent to his parents and the documents from the schools. He took on a bigger administrative role than most applicants, completing all the forms, sending testing, and coordinating with his teachers—all from his dorm room.

Rasul's application list included eight of the most selective schools in the United States, including two schools who had sent admissions associates to London that fall for school fairs and interviews. Rasul was excited to schedule meetings with them, taking the day off from school and making the two-hour train trip to London alone. He found the hotel, checked in with the front desk, and was met in the lobby for each of his interviews. I was impressed since I knew that most of my eighth-grade clients would need parental help for this type of meeting. Rasul had an especially good meeting with an admissions dean from St. Paul's School. He followed up with his interviewer throughout the admissions year, sending him email updates about his progress and asking questions about the school.

Rasul was accepted at St. Paul's and wait-listed or denied at the other schools on his list. He was thrilled with the opportunity and became an active member of the St. Paul's community, trying new sports and activities and finding leadership roles, friends, and mentors. After graduation, Rasul went on to Boston University and continued his dream of thriving in the United States.

The ideal international population at boarding school is a mix of students from many different countries. If the community has more than 10 percent of the student population from any one country, it can lead to students forming cliques, not speaking English, and not getting the most out of their experience. Students from countries with many applicants, such as China, will have a harder time in admissions than students from countries in Europe and other places with fewer applicants. I worked with a student from Sweden, a top skier in his country, who wanted to have an American high school experience. He was admitted to every school to which he had applied, both because of his ability to contribute to the ski team and also because of his unique cultural background.

CHINESE STUDENTS IN BOARDING SCHOOL

Students in China face enormous competition for university enrollment and for employment after graduation. They study intensely for a year or longer before undergoing a two-day national test called the *gaokao*, which is the sole determinant for university admissions. Last year, almost thirteen million Chinese students took the *gaokao* with hopes of landing a spot in a Chinese university.[2] This test-based system pushes many Chinese families to consider high school and college abroad, where their child can be evaluated for university admission on more than just one test. This, as well as other factors, leads Chinese students to apply to US boarding schools in great numbers.

Because boarding schools have a limit on the number of students they will admit from any one country, students from China face more difficult odds. For example, at Northfield Mt. Hermon, they receive about 250 applications from China and will admit fewer than eight each year. Frederick Gunn receives over 150 applicants from China and accepts four boys and four girls in the ninth grade. They will only accept a tenth grader if a student from China leaves the school, and they don't admit new Chinese students into the eleventh grade. At Cranbrook, they receive over 200 applications a year from China and will accept nine applicants to enroll just eight students. The yield is very high because admissions directors are in contact with consultants to ask about the student's first choice. In order to yield the eight students they hope to enroll, admissions does not accept a large number of students. These acceptance rates average less than 5 percent, which makes it one of the most difficult admission environments in the United States.

Many successful boarding school applicants come from junior boarding schools, where they spend their middle school years improving their English and proving that they can excel in an American boarding school. Other Chinese families consider day schools that either offer host families or a small boarding program.

WHAT ADMISSIONS COMMITTEES LOOK FOR

A large part of the admissions evaluation is the same as it is for domestic students. They are looking at grades, testing, teacher recommendations, essays, and interview reports to gain a picture of the student and how she will thrive at their school. Some schools require English fluency, and others don't, providing language support instead.

Caralyn Dea, director of international recruitment at Frederick Gunn, looks closely at candidates:

Gunn is looking for students who are open minded and hardworking because we want them to get the most out of their time at Gunn. We also want students that will significantly impact the community. If they have the aim of going to a US university, then we are equally focused on their academics, athletics/arts, and community involvement. They are treated entirely like a domestic candidate when we are reading their files and discussing their candidacy.[3]

Metta Dael, director of international admission at Northfield Mt. Hermon, advises,

I look for three things in domestic and international candidates. The first is that they don't *only* have a *perfect* academic profile. If they only have strong academics to show in their profile and are not involved in other things, they will typically have a hard time adjusting to boarding school, where they are required to be involved in multiple ways in the community. The second thing that I look at is the type of activities a student is engaged in. Are they just taking instrumental lessons, or are they a part of an orchestra? Are they taking tennis lessons or a part of a soccer team? The latter are activities that are built on building relationships with others versus doing things individually. Lastly, I look at students' resilience. I try to learn about how they have responded to challenges. Most importantly, I look to see if a student has failed something. How did they react? If a student is not afraid of failing, then I know they are going to try new things. How amazing to be on an adventure like boarding school that is filled with things to try both academically, within extracurriculars, through social relationships, etc.[4]

TIPS ON THRIVING AT BOARDING SCHOOL

It's important for international students to find an ally and form a strong personal connection with at least one adult on campus. This is good advice for domestic students as well, but for teens from abroad, who are far away from home and undergoing a cultural adjustment, an adult mentor can be a key part of their success. In the boarding school world, it is very easy to find this type of relationship, particularly for students who actively look for it. Schools are full of caring adults, so students should look to their houseparents, coaches, advisors, or teachers and try to connect with at least one of them. Upperclassmen can help to smooth the way for new international students, and they may be assigned to one in a peer leader group or big-sibling partnership, or they may become friends with older students through life in the dorms.

Boarding school concierge services are private companies that help international parents support their children who are attending school far from home. They can meet students at the airport and assist with move-in, transportation to doctor's appointments, or activities off campus, as well as many of the day-to-day aspects of school life. The staff is available for emergencies, including suspensions and expulsions, when a student may be asked to leave campus immediately. Many boarding schools recommend these services for students who don't have family or friends in the United States, and some schools require students to have a "guardian" who is able to get to campus within one day to assist in an emergency or disciplinary case. Concierge services also offer housing or student trips during school vacations, college visit trips, and birthday- and graduation-party planning. Student Concierge Services (http://scshereforyou.com/), Student Health Services (https://studenthealthadvocates.com/), and Boston Concierge Support Service (https://bostoncss.com/) are examples of firms that offer fee-based services for international students.

Caralyn Dea offers valuable advice to new international students:

> If you want to thrive, then try everything! Do as much as you can each day, and be open to different perspectives and experiences. Being an international student comes with a different set of personal responsibilities than if you were a domestic student. Your parents have given you the gift of not only education but education abroad so that you may grow, learn, and develop in a

different way than your peers in your home country. When you try new things, you learn new skills and make more friends. Your social group grows and you have more experiences and more fun. There is no point going to school in a different country if students are only going to sit in their room and study. The American boarding school system is intentionally designed to be experiential, so experience as much as you can!

Metta Dael suggests, "Set up times to chat with your parents so you don't have to absorb and navigate their nervousness and worry. Bring snacks from home, whether it be ramen or chocolate that you love—those things can be really soothing when you're homesick. And it is okay to take a time out when orientation or the first few weeks get really overwhelming. Go on a walk, find a quiet place to read, or recharge with a good movie on your computer—just take some alone time."

DAY SCHOOL WITH HOMESTAY

Day schools that have the ability to issue an I-20 form for student visas offer a strong alternative to traditional boarding schools. These schools offer host family accommodations or a dormitory for a small number of students who are welcomed into their community of local students. They partner with companies that help recruit international students and provide application support and assistance with selecting a host family.

The benefits of the day school programs are that they are less expensive, they are easier to get into, and they offer instruction for students who are not yet fluent in English. Some parents are skeptical about the homestay accommodation and are concerned that it is not a true boarding school experience, as they are missing the evening study hall, weekend activities, and boarding culture. But for some students, the day school option offers their best chance to get to America, improve their English, and reach their educational goals.

Examples of day schools with host family programs for international students include Immaculate High School and Williams School in Connecticut; Bishop Montgomery, Mater Dei, and Justin Siena High in California; Morris Catholic High School and Union Catholic High School in New Jersey; St. Anthony's in New York; St. Edward's School and Melbourne Catholic High School in Florida; St. John Bosco in Idaho; St. Thomas Aquinas High School in New Hampshire; and Cape Cod Academy and Waring School in Massachusetts.

Schools that have a small boarding program that comprises mostly international students include Michigan Lutheran; Wisconsin Lutheran; North Cross School in Virginia; Fryeburg and Washington Academy in Maine; Lyndon Institute in Vermont; Chaminade in Missouri; Cotter School, St. John's Prep, and St. Croix School in Minnesota; the International School of Minnesota; St. Stanislaus in Mississippi; Maur Hill in Kansas; St. Bede's in Illinois; North Cedar Academy and St. Lawrence Seminary in Wisconsin; Sun Valley Community School and Riverstone International in Idaho; and Hilton Head Prep in South Carolina.

Parents who are considering a day school and homestay for their child often start with a company that helps families find a good academic and student life fit. Companies that match students with schools and homestays include Amerigo Education (https://www.amerigoeducation.com/), Cambridge Network (https://www.cambridgenetwork.com/), and Educatius (https://www.educatius.org).

12

Students with Learning Disabilities or ADHD at Boarding Schools

It is difficult for parents to see their children struggle in school. Poor grades and problems with attentiveness and organization often lead to the frustration that plagues many teenagers and causes strife for the whole family. Some parents have been dealing with their children's academic problems for many years, having tried tutors or accommodations and support in their local schools. Others find that the complexities of middle school brought new academic challenges their students had not experienced before.

One solution for these students is an academic support program at certain boarding schools. Many of my clients have had life-changing experiences where they built academic skills and grew in self-confidence while seeing improved grades. When I describe boarding school support programs to my clients, one of the first things they ask is whether programs like this exist at their local day schools. While there are some day schools that offer structured learning support within a college prep curriculum, it's not common. However, many boarding schools successfully combine a rigorous academic program with AP and honors courses along with a learning support program staffed by experienced learning specialists. Parents who may not have initially considered boarding school often change their mind when they discover how this environment can help their child succeed and emerge college ready.

WHAT IS LEARNING SUPPORT?

First, it's important to understand the level of extra help that is available to all students and is included in the cost of tuition at most boarding schools. Students can go to teachers for extra help, work with peer tutors, and attend sessions in the school writing center or math lab. The evening study hours include a quiet, social media–free time with teachers on duty, checking in to ensure that students are working. At some boarding schools, students do not have to self-advocate, meaning that teachers will approach the students and ask them to come for extra review or to work on a second draft of a paper with the teacher's help. This type of nurturing, academically focused boarding school community is sometimes all that is needed to help a student excel.

But there are some students who need more support and will only find success when they participate in a structured academic support program. They may benefit from one-on-one sessions with a learning specialist or subject specialist. This level of support can be found either at a boarding school that is entirely focused on students with learning disabilities or ADHD or at a traditional school that offers a learning support program for a small percentage of the student body.

Learning support varies by school, so parents should evaluate the options. Fee-based support often includes one-on-one sessions or group sessions with a learning specialist after school. The focus could be remediation of reading problems, organization, review of what was taught in class that day, or help with note-taking, time management, and writing. Time spent with the learning support team is not only used to go over homework but for students to build skills that will help them become confident learners.

The first step is to consider your child and his needs. If your student is struggling, consider whether the concerns are medical, emotional, or academic issues. Would he benefit simply from attending a nurturing boarding school with a dedicated evening study session and opportunities for extra help? Or does he need an individual plan that includes one-on-one time with learning specialists? Parents should evaluate their child's grades, test results, and attitude toward school but also their level of independence. The goal is to help them achieve in school now but also for them to be ready to work independently in college.

NEUROPSYCHOLOGICAL EVALUATIONS

An important tool in evaluating your child and her academic support needs is a neuropsychological exam. Neuropsychology is the study of the relationship between the brain and behavior, and a neuropsychological evaluation is a test of how the brain functions. This evaluation helps parents and educators understand a child's cognitive, social, and emotional needs. It's administered by a psychologist or neuropsychologist primarily outside of school, although some public school districts offer this type of testing. This one-on-one test is administered for a few hours at a time over several days. A student will answer questions that test his attention and memory in addition to questions related to his social-emotional profile. Parents will be asked questions about their child's developmental history and about the family's mental health history. After the evaluation, the parents are given a lengthy report that may or may not include a diagnosis of a learning disability, an attention deficit, or a processing issue. The report may include recommendations for academics, therapy, and school accommodations. Common diagnoses that I see on a report include ADHD, processing speed issues, working memory problems, dyslexia, and anxiety or depression.

The neuropsychological exam (e.g., WISC-V) is a tool that helps parents understand their child's needs and how to support them in their educational journey. The admissions team and learning support staff also use the test when evaluating applicants. Although parents are sometimes reluctant to share the report with prospective schools, it is actually a crucial part of the process of evaluating a student and arranging support. When an applicant submits their neuropsychological report to a boarding school admissions office, it will be shared with the learning support team at the school. If approved, both the family and the school can be confident that it is an academic match and the student will thrive.

At Forman, a school specializing in ADHD and dyslexia support, evaluations are required to be submitted before the campus visit, as indicated on their website: "Along with the application form, please submit educational testing given within the last three years. We require testing prior to scheduling a campus visit and interview. Testing must include measures of cognitive ability such as a WISC/WAIS test as well as measures of achievement such as WJ-IV or WIAT-III."[1]

LEARNING SUPPORT PROGRAMS

Students with diagnosed learning differences, such as dyslexia, dysgraphia, expressive language disorder, or ADHD, often learn best in schools that have a learning support center and a school culture of support. These programs help students to close the gap between their current level of achievement and their potential. Some of these students are drawn to traditional college prep schools that have a small percentage of their students enrolled in a learning support program. This experience allows the students to participate in advanced courses, be part of a bright and motivated peer group, and attend schools with a variety of activities and types of learners while also being part of a dedicated program for learning support. At most of these schools, only about 15 percent to 20 percent of the students receive learning support, with most graduating from the program within a year or two. There is usually an added fee for learning support, although some schools, such as Canterbury, have a learning support program included in the cost of tuition.

The Center for Academic Excellence at Frederick Gunn School is staffed with five full-time learning specialists who meet with students individually during the school day. This coaching, which requires an extra fee, includes subject-specific support, reading skill development, study skills, and executive functioning support. Erin Brown, codirector of the Center for Academic Excellence, says, "The purpose of the learning support program at Gunn is not to earn specific grades, it's to develop strategies and skills and for students to understand themselves as learners, and for them to become better self-advocates. The skills that we work on are lifelong skills, which they will need throughout their lifetime."[2]

Kents Hill School offers a program with three different levels of support that "balance academic tutoring with individualized instruction to build advocacy, awareness, confidence, and resilience."[3] The levels of support include one-on-one, two-to-one, or small group instruction, although each student also receives an individualized learning plan and open-door support during free time and evening study hours.

Trinity Pawling has a long and successful history of offering support to students with dyslexia, language-based learning disabilities, or executive functioning challenges. The Center for Learning Achievement "gives students the strategic support and proven skills that lead to academic independence and intellectual empowerment."[4] Students in the LEAD (Learning through Enrichment, Analysis, and Development) program take three courses over two years in addition to their regular course work. The classes use a modified Orton-Gillingham approach and cover the topics of reading comprehension, composition, and analytical writing. The program has changed the lives of many boys, giving them both the skills and the confidence to excel in college.

The well-regarded learning support program at Kimball Union offers an individual tutorial, a structured study tutorial with a small group, and subject-specific instruction.

Rectory, a junior boarding school for students in grades 5–9, offers an individualized instruction program, which is a scheduled course in the academic day. They offer support for students with learning differences, including ADHD, working memory and processing disorders, and executive functioning deficits. Students in the Roxbury Academic Support Program at Cheshire Academy benefit from learning-strategy instruction, goal setting, and progress monitoring as they build academic skills. Once students at Cheshire have improved and gained confidence, they can move from comprehensive support to the standard level.

Winchendon School has an excellent learning support program and several alumni success stories that show just how far students with learning challenges can go. Bryan Perla was a student in the Hatch Learning Support Program at Winchendon for three years. He was a top gymnast outside of school and went on to attend Stanford University, where he competed on their men's gymnastics team.

While at Winchendon, Perla designed, prototyped, and produced a product that helps with gift wrapping. He went on *Shark Tank*, a TV show competition, and received two offers; he then made a deal with one of the "shark" investors. Today Perla is a Stanford graduate and the CEO of Little Elf, the company he founded. The Little Elf website credits Perla's background as a key part of his success: "Perla soon learned that, when embraced, dyslexic thinkers have unique brilliance to share. He was taught about big-picture thinking, how to visualize complex problems, and identifying needs in the world in order to help others. This led to Perla's passion for inventions at a young age."[5] Perla also benefited from attending Winchendon, a school that supported him as a learner and encouraged him to reach his goals.

Other schools with strong learning support programs include Brewster, Dublin, Gould, Grier, Hoosac, Lawrence, Marvelwood, New Hampton, St. Andrew's of Rhode Island, Tilton, and many others.

It's also important to note that every boarding school offers learning support of some kind, even schools that typically enroll high-achieving students. For example, Milton Academy, a selective school, has the Academic Skills Center (ASC), which is staffed by learning specialists and serves students for regularly scheduled meetings or for drop-in help. The ASC matches students with peer tutors; arranges accommodations, such as extra time for taking the ACT or SAT; and offers instruction in organization, note-taking, study strategies, and time management. The ASC staff members coach students on meeting their goals and help connect them with teachers, tutors, or counselors when needed. At Phillips Exeter, a school known for its academic rigor, the Learning Center is open every Monday through Thursday night and offers individual help to students free of charge. Teachers and peer tutors offer help in writing, math, and science.

LEARNING SUPPORT–SPECIALIZED BOARDING SCHOOLS

Some students with learning differences want to be part of a school community where they know they aren't alone, where they have a big peer group of students who are also working hard to overcome their challenges. There are boarding schools that specifically serve students with ADHD or learning disabilities. They have small class sizes, sometimes with only four or five students, and innovative teaching styles that lead to lively, engaging classrooms. The curriculum includes reading instruction and remedial work for those who need it. Beyond academics, they are typical boarding schools, offering full programs in athletics and the arts. Let's examine some examples of excellent learning support schools.

Eagle Hill is a supportive community that offers a rigorous International Baccalaureate diploma program while also providing well-respected support programs in speech, language, and reading. This mix of support and rigor is ideal for bright students who have yet to reach their potential.

The reading program at Eagle Hill has been described by a staff member as broad and helpful to all types of students: "If a student needs remedial help in reading, he or she will be scheduled into a reading tutorial, reading fluency class, or reading development class if the need is in word attack skills or fluency. Reading approaches that are used include Orton-Gillingham, Wilson Reading System, Lindamood LiPS, and Structured Word Inquiry. If the remedial need is in reading comprehension, the student will be scheduled into a reading comprehension class such as Close Reading Strategies for Fiction, Expository Reading Comprehension, or Comprehension Imagery."[6]

Forman is a coed school specializing in ADHD and dyslexia support. When I visited campus, I saw students who were interested and involved and teachers who were moving around the classroom, engaging with each student. Forman teachers are specialists who receive ongoing professional development and are trained to meet each student where they are. It creates a vibrant learning community, aligning with the Forman approach, which says, "You learn differently, so we teach differently."

Landmark is another school for students with dyslexia or language-based learning disabilities, but the school also has a unique program designed for each student: "The cornerstone of the Landmark Approach is the daily one-to-one tutorial personalized for each student."[7] Landmark also has small classes, an advisor system, and highly trained teachers.

The Woodhall School serves bright boys who have not found success in traditional school environments. Matt Woodhall, head of school, says,

Often our boys have a learning style that is difficult to categorize. Their struggles have affected not only their school performance but also their relationships with their peers, teachers, and family. We take an individualized approach to address the needs of the whole boy: his intellectual, physical, emotional, and spiritual growth. We recognize that we need to make each student feel safe and valued and competent. At Woodhall, boys learn how to build relationships, take accountability, and establish a greater sense of self and ownership in their education and life.[8]

Hampshire Country School enrolls boys in middle school who are bright but may not have been successful in school, often due to neurodevelopmental delays. According to their mission statement, the school "offers understanding, lightheartedness, and structure to educate students in a family-style, supportive, and calming learning community."[9] Students usually stay at Hampshire for three years, with many then moving on to traditional high schools.

Other learning support boarding schools include Brehm, Curry Ingram, Gow, Greenwood, Maplebrook, Middlebridge, Oxford, Riverview, Rock Point, and Vanguard.

LEARNING SUPPORT SUCCESS STORIES

Jenny, age thirteen, wanted to do well in school, but she was often disappointed in her grades. It took her a long time to get through her homework at night, and she always needed extra time on tests and assignments. She was often late to class, disorganized, and she made careless mistakes in her school work. She hated it when her teachers called them "careless mistakes" because she really did care, and she couldn't help making mistakes. Jenny considered herself to be shy, yet she also talked too much when she was nervous and wasn't always the best listener. Jenny's parents noticed these wrinkles in her learning profile and decided to get her evaluated by a neuropsychologist.

After the multiday evaluation, Jenny's parents received a diagnosis and recommendation. Jenny had ADHD and a slow processing speed, but her IQ was high, and her evaluation showed that she was strong in many areas. Jenny's parents felt encouraged that her academic problems were defined, and they were taking the first steps toward getting her help. They began to consider boarding schools as an option.

An educational consultant recommended Cushing Academy and described a recent student who had made tremendous gains in academic results and confidence. Jenny and her parents visited the campus and met with the soccer coach and the learning center director. Although they had planned to visit other schools, their visit to Cushing went so well that they decided to apply to just this one school.

Jenny enrolled at Cushing and had the best academic year of her life. Frequent sessions with her learning support coach helped her to develop her reading and writing skills, and her executive functioning coach helped her with strategies related to organization. Her grades went up, and for the first time, Jenny felt that she could succeed. After four years at Cushing, Jenny graduated and enrolled at Northeastern University, where she majored in business and felt well prepared for college academics.

Lucio was an eighth grader who attended Windward, a K–8 school for children with dyslexia. He had faced struggles with reading from a young age, but with the support he received at Windward, he developed the strategies to excel in school. While evaluating high schools, Lucio's parents were unsure if he still needed learning support. He was a strong reader and had a desire to take advanced courses, but they realized that Lucio may need some academic support, at least at the beginning of high school.

Lucio considered Canterbury, Williston Northampton, and Millbrook. His parents submitted his neuropsychological evaluation to each school and spoke with the learning support teams. They felt confident that any of those schools could support Lucio. In the end, it was Lucio who chose the school that was right for him, a decision he based on his interactions with the faculty and students as well as his evaluation of sports, arts, and campus life. He chose Williston Northampton and started with their Academic Strategies Tutorial program where he met with a small group and an instructor each week. With strong grades, solid work habits, and confidence in himself, Lucio started his sophomore year without any learning support. He continued to use the drop-in writing and math centers, and he frequently went to teachers for extra help. He also worked with subject specific tutors for challenging courses such as chemistry, algebra 2, and precalculus. Lucio graduated with high grades and enrolled at George Washington University.

THERAPEUTIC BOARDING SCHOOLS

Parents who are concerned about their teenagers' social and emotional well-being often consider boarding schools that have a clinical component. Years ago, the obvious choice would be a therapeutic boarding school, which has around-the-clock support with group, individual, and family therapy and a focus on developing skills and confidence. But there has been a lot of change in the therapeutic world recently, and many schools have closed or transitioned into residential treatment centers. This is a more profitable business model since residential treatment centers can accept health insurance payments, while therapeutic boarding schools generally cannot.

Parents today can decide between the small number of therapeutic boarding schools that still exist, or they can consider what Krissy Naspo, educational consultant with the Bertram Group, calls "soft landing schools." These are boarding schools that offer therapy, support, and a focus on developing healthy relationships, all while being part of a traditional high school campus community and a general college prep program. Students in need of this lower level of counseling support benefit from being with a peer group similar to what you would find in any high school. These are not therapeutic schools but regular boarding schools, though these have the capacity to accept a small number of students who need this level of support in order to succeed.

"My students have thrived at soft landing schools," explains Krissy Naspo, "These schools offer the support and counseling needed to keep the student moving forward and feeling successful. The kids benefit from the structured school day with academics, sports, or arts activities, and they love being part of the school community."[10]

Therapeutic schools are different from traditional boarding schools in several ways. They operate all year, with students enrolling at any time. Some students stay and graduate, while others return to their home school after their goals have been met. Therapeutic schools are more expensive than traditional boarding schools and often charge by the month. They are staffed not only with teachers and coaches but also nurses, psychologists, and clinical staff.

It's important for families to get qualified advice when selecting a therapeutic boarding school or when considering a soft landing school for their child. When I get inquiries from families who need a therapeutic placement, I refer them to consultants who are experienced in this area. These are professionals who visit programs, have extensive professional contacts in the field, and have many years of experience placing students in therapeutic schools and programs.

Two examples of therapeutic boarding schools are Grove School and Glenholme School, both located in Connecticut. The National Association of Therapeutic Schools and Programs, (https://natsap.org) and All Kinds of Therapy (www.allkindsoftherapy.com) are good resources for parents who want to learn more about therapeutic options for their children.

13

Postgraduates at Boarding Schools

There are currently about one thousand high school graduates enrolled in boarding schools in a fifth year of course work, which is referred to as a postgraduate year, or a PG year. This is a year of structured independence, offering students the chance to live in a supportive residential environment while they build study skills, improve grades, and gain the maturity needed to be successful in college. It's also a common strategy for athletes who hope to play their sport in college and benefit from an extra year or a chance to improve their recruiting results. Moreover, the boarding component helps to ease the transition to college life and is a key element of the PG year.

Jake was a young man who finally started to "get it" at the end of his junior year. His early high school grades had been a collection of Cs, which didn't bother him much at the time. During eleventh grade, though, he started to realize that his grades would affect his future, and he found that with a little effort, he was able to do well.

"I wish I had another year of high school to show the colleges that I am not a C student," he said at the time. He needed to improve his writing, retake the SAT, and post better grades. Jake enrolled in the PG year program at Cheshire Academy.

Not only did his grades improve, but so did his self-confidence and ability to function independently. He frequently went for extra help and was able to build on the upward grade trend that started at the end of his junior year. He was admitted to the University of Massachusetts, his first choice, and most importantly, he was prepared for and ready to thrive at college.

Brady wanted to play basketball at a top academic college and was willing to try anything to make his dream come true. He was a talented player and a strong student, ranked at the top of his class at his large suburban high school. He played for a club team and started on the varsity team at his high school. Like many top athletes, Brady had experienced some ups and downs. His club coach had favorites, and Brady wasn't one of them. He also had a nagging knee injury that slowed him down at times.

Brady received two offers to play college basketball, but they were at colleges that were not academically strong or selective. Brady decided to do a PG year and go back into the recruiting pool for another try. He enrolled at Millbrook and was challenged academically while he worked hard on the basketball court. By the fall of his PG year, Brady had received several offers from colleges on his target list. Brady committed to Bowdoin, an academic powerhouse school with a strong basketball program, and explained, "Not only did the PG year help me get here, but it helped me to manage the time constraints and pressure of both playing basketball and studying at a high level."

Brady and Jake are students with very different profiles, but both were successful in their PG year programs. More than just a "do-over" option, the PG year varies greatly by school and offers an excellent gap year option in preparation for college.

WHAT IS THE PG YEAR?

The PG year is an additional year of high school course work that is taken after a student graduates from high school but before he enrolls in college. It is intended for students who have not yet applied to college or for those who were not successful in the college admissions process. Students build study skills, improve their writing technique, and take an entire year of college prep classes, all in a supportive and structured environment.

At most schools the PG students are simply new members of the senior class. They can fully participate in sports, activities, and in the social life of the school. They live in dorms with underclassmen and receive diplomas from the school at graduation. They are subject to the same rules and curfews as the seniors.

Like with any other journey, the result of the PG year depends on where the student was when he started. Some students emerge from the PG year more confident, with better study skills and a feeling that they can be successful in college. They often find themselves admitted to colleges that may previously have been out of reach. Many young athletes find that the PG year gives them time to grow physically and emotionally, improve in their sports, and get attention from college coaches. Simply stated, the PG year gives a student the gift of time. It allows a student one more year to build academic and athletic skills and to get ready for the demands of college.

HISTORY OF THE PG YEAR

Young men have been attending PG year programs at boarding schools for over sixty years. The first students were sponsored by US service academies, which ordered them to a year of prep school before accepting them as cadets and midshipmen. Even today, the US Naval Academy Foundation sponsors about seventy PG year students at select boarding schools, giving them a year of preparation before entering the US Naval Academy.

The early PG programs were not entirely full of military types, though, at the time, they usually fit the same mold:

they were young men who needed an improved academic transcript either to play on a sports team or to join a service academy class. It was a year of structure or foundation that arrived, for many of them, at just the right time in their lives. Several boarding schools today note that their boards of trustees include at least one PG graduate. Those young men who did not have their lives completely together at age eighteen often went on to find great success in life, and they give back to their schools financially and through volunteer work.

The PG year is still chosen by significantly more boys than girls. A typical New England boarding school that has fifteen PG students is likely to have two or three PG girls, and in some years, they may have no girls at all. The imbalance prevails because girls typically have fewer concerns about maturity and independence, and they don't benefit as much from the athletic component, since they aren't likely to gain physical size at that age. From a social point of view, boys tend to welcome a year in which they are the oldest in the high school environment, whereas that feature typically holds less appeal for girls.

THE ATHLETIC PG YEAR

Sports are very important to some young adults today, and these individuals will give almost anything to make it to the holy grail of college athletics. For many boys, a PG year with the right coach and increased exposure can help them reach their goal of playing intercollegiate athletics, as the extra time and practice sessions with other top athletes can help them make that move to the next level in their sport.

For example, an eighteen-year-old boy who is deemed too small for Division 1 football may grow large enough during his PG year to attract the attention of coaches who passed him over the previous year. A basketball hopeful might gain a few inches in that time, as well as benefit from working out with other top players. Dedicated athletes who are looking for a place to shine and to potentially be noticed by college coaches often meet their goals in a PG program.

Athletic programs vary greatly from school to school. Serious contenders for Division 1 football can attend the PG football team at Fork Union, a school that boasts two Heisman trophy winners, twelve National Football League (NFL) first-round draft picks, and over seventy graduates in the NFL. The PG football team plays college teams and a few high school teams in their fall season. Basketball players are drawn to Hargrave, Blair, Lawrenceville, New Hampton, or Brewster, each with graduates in the NBA. IMG is a sports-oriented school with opportunities for PGs in many different sports.

One of my clients was a baseball player named Dakota, who played for a highly ranked public school in Texas. He called me in March of his senior year when he was reconsidering his college commitment. He had cast his college recruiting net wide but was not offered a spot by any of the Division 1 colleges on his radar. He committed to a Division 3 college near Boston, applied, and was accepted, then sent a deposit to attend. But his dream of playing Ivy League baseball was strong, and he felt that he was very close to getting an offer and that, with a little more time, he could achieve his goal. He reached out to a few of the Ivy League coaches who he had spoken to the year before, and they encouraged Dakota to reclass and try again. This meant rejoining his baseball club team in his reclassed year, plus attending summer showcases and college prospect camps.

I worked with Dakota on finding a PG year program, and he was accepted to several despite applying after the deadline. With Dakota's strong grades and baseball prospects, he had the choice of several good schools. He was accepted to Lawrenceville in April, decommitted from the Division 3 college he had planned to attend, and spent the summer on the baseball circuit, trying to get an offer from an Ivy League college. He joined the PG year program at Lawrenceville in September, and within two weeks, he had received an offer from Cornell to play baseball. He was thrilled with the result and enjoyed his PG year before heading to Cornell.

THE POSTGRADUATE YEAR ADMISSIONS PROCESS

People are often surprised at how much work goes into the PG year application. Students follow the same application process as regular boarding school applicants, which means completing essays, interviews, and testing, as well as submitting a graded paper or writing sample.

Although the interview is a formality in college admissions, it is a crucial part of the PG year application. The admissions office uses the interview as a means to get to know a student and his accomplishments and to address any academic concerns. They also use the interview to gauge the student's willingness and interest in doing a PG year. Faculty members do not want a miserable student on their campus, so they pay close attention to whether the PG year fits in the student's overall education plan and whether they feel he would adapt to the structured environment.

The application time line varies. It is recommended that students apply to PG programs at the same time their classmates are applying to colleges. Many students apply to both PG programs and colleges. Selective schools have a deadline of January 15 with a notification date of March 10. If accepted, the student will be invited to a Revisit Day to help him decide if the PG year is the right decision for him.

The PG applicant is known to come late to the process, so schools often have openings through the spring. If a student is unhappy with her college choices in April, there is still a good chance that she can find a spot in a PG year class. Less selective PG programs see the bulk of their PG applicants start the process in the spring. Bridgton Academy, an all PG boarding program, has rolling admissions.

IMPLICATIONS OF PURSUING A PG YEAR

Students who need "the gift of time" will find that the PG year can be enormously beneficial. A foundation year before college particularly benefits boys, as they often become more motivated and organized during the later years of high school.

The director of college counseling at a boarding school with a twenty-student PG program says, "The PG year is a great opportunity for late bloomers or students who have started to be successful at the end of their high school career. But they need a commitment to be a student and they must be able to hit the ground running when they get to campus. A good year can be very beneficial, but a bad academic experience can be a real step backward."

There is little flexibility in leaving a PG year program if it doesn't work out. There is no public school to return to, so changing your mind about the PG year and leaving in the middle of the semester can have a disastrous effect on college admissions. This is why it is important for candidates to visit campuses and talk with faculty and students: they need to determine whether a PG year is right for them.

One of the drawbacks of doing a PG year is the expense. The tuition, which costs as much as $75,000 at many boarding schools and $45,000 at military and other lower-priced schools, is a hefty fee for an academic year offering no college credit. Financial aid is available to those who qualify, but schools tend to be less generous with financial aid for PG students, as they are on campus for only one year.

Many parents consider a reclass junior year as an alternative to the PG year. Rather than graduating from high school and then spending one year as a PG, their student can reclass after junior year, spending two years at boarding school. This plan, although more expensive, offers the student more time to benefit from the boarding school experience. PG students must start the college application process as soon as they arrive on campus, while those reclassing after eleventh grade have a full academic year to adjust to the school and show their positive gains before the college process begins.

PG YEAR OPTIONS

There are over one hundred boarding schools that offer a PG year program. Parents can evaluate the schools and consider how PGs are integrated into the campus community. Some students prefer schools with a large PG year cohort of fifteen or more students, while others are okay joining a school as the only PG student or as one of just two or three. Girls may prefer PG programs with a history of enrolling several female students each year. Bridgton Academy is an all-PG year, all-boys school, which students may prefer because of its larger PG age cohort and ability to arrange college credit. Parents and students should consider the campus culture and academic preparation for college, which they can find out about through online research, campus visits, and conversations with faculty, students, and coaches.

The following is a selection of schools with PG year programs: Andover, Avon Old Farms, Berkshire, Blair, Bolles, Brewster, Bridgton, Canterbury, Cheshire, Choate, Cushing, Darlington, Deerfield, Exeter, Fork Union, Forman, Frederick Gunn, Hargrave, Hill, Holderness, Hoosac, Hun, IMG, Kent, Kents Hill, Kimball Union, Lawrenceville, Loomis, Mercersburg, Montverde, New Hampton, NMH, Pomfret, Proctor, Putney, St. Thomas More, Salisbury, Shattuck St. Mary's, Suffield, Taft, Tilton, Trinity Pawling, Westminster, Wilbraham and Monson, Williston Northampton, and Western Reserve.

III

TYPES OF BOARDING SCHOOLS

14

✢

Ultraselective Boarding Schools

Ultraselective schools have a certain cache, they enjoy name recognition around the world, and they represent a brand that is synonymous with success and prestige. These schools draw applications from talented and accomplished students, and they could fill their incoming classes several times over with excellent candidates. They are called elite and ultraselective and have been labeled "top schools," as they deny the majority of applicants who apply. Although there are hundreds of boarding schools in the United States, it is this group of approximately twenty ultraselective schools that people are the most curious about and most interested in attending.

For some families, their path is "ultraselective or bust," meaning that they will either enroll their student in a top school or they will keep them home to attend a local public or private school. The interest in ultraselective schools has grown in recent years, just as it has grown with Ivy League and other elite colleges. Many people consider these boarding schools and colleges to be part of a unique path to success in life. There is a belief that a diploma from these institutions opens doors and that the experiences and connections made are unrivaled. But are these elite schools truly different at their core? Do they have offerings or opportunities that other schools do not? Let's examine this type of boarding school and the things to consider when evaluating them for your child.

WHICH SCHOOLS ARE ULTRASELECTIVE?

If you were to define ultraselective schools by acceptance rate only, this group would include schools that accept fewer than 20 percent of applicants, with several of them accepting fewer than 10 percent of those who apply. This includes the old guard schools, which have been prestigious and exclusive for two hundred years, along with those that have achieved their selective status more recently.

"St. Grottlesex" is an old term that is a blend of the names of five New England boarding schools—St. Paul's, St. Mark's, St. George's, Groton, and Middlesex—and was used to refer to a school experience that was wealthy, Christian, and elite. Those schools were known to be among the country's most prestigious, along with Andover, Exeter, Choate, Deerfield, Lawrenceville, Milton, and Hotchkiss.

Today, these schools are diverse, welcoming students from different socioeconomic backgrounds and from many different states and countries around the world. For example, at Choate, 42 percent of the student body are domestic students of color and Choate students come from thirty-eight states and fifty-two countries.

Today some of these boarding schools have formed a group called the Ten Schools Admissions Organization, which is essentially a coalition for marketing and collaboration. The Ten Schools, including Choate, Deerfield, Hill, Hotchkiss, Lawrenceville, Loomis Chaffee, Andover, Exeter, St. Paul's, and Taft, is a group of peer schools that host school fairs, virtual information sessions, and other opportunities to market their schools to a wide audience. The Ten Schools Admission

Organization was founded in 1952 as a "group of top ten New England college preparatory institutions that cooperate in their outreach to prospective students and their families. Our goal is to guide prospective families on their journey to find the most suitable secondary boarding school experience and to bring better understanding of boarding school education and its benefits."[1]

Other selective schools on the East Coast include Blair, Concord, St. Andrew's of Delaware, Peddie, and Westminster, and on the West Coast, Cate and Thacher.

WHAT'S UNIQUE ABOUT ULTRASELECTIVE SCHOOLS

Boarding schools are all about the people, and at the ultraselective schools, the admissions team is able to carefully craft an exceptional campus community. My students who have attended these schools have told me they love being a part of a community where everyone is a good student and everyone participates and tries hard at school. They benefit from being around teenagers who are accomplished in sports or the arts, as well as from those who come from different cultures and backgrounds. And since ultraselective schools screen for personality and the ability to work and live with others, the students at these schools tend to be friendly, open, and engaging, which makes for an excellent high school experience.

There are also classes, activities, and experiences that students at the ultraselective schools have that are difficult to find at other schools throughout the world. While many of the things they do are common to students at all high schools, such as taking algebra 2 or playing on a junior varsity soccer team, there are a variety of unique opportunities.

To start, Phillips Exeter has an underwater robotics club. It's called Murex, and the students describe it on their website, writing, "Calling upon our foundation of innovative, open source electrical engineering designs, we push the absolute limits of modern day robotics."[2]

The team competes regionally and at the world championships.

Exeter's curriculum offers classes not found at most high schools. Students who want to study Greek or Latin can earn a classical diploma. Not only do they offer the typical French and Spanish classes, but they also have courses in Arabic, Chinese, Japanese, German, and Russian. Math goes beyond the calculus level found in most high schools, advancing to linear algebra and multivariable calculus. Exeter offers classes such as Malaria: Exploring Bioinformatics and Next Generation Sequencing, Sports Science, Principles of Engineering and Design, and War, Identity, and Nationhood of the United States.

Students at Exeter can study abroad during the fall, winter, or spring term at destinations including England, France, Japan, China, Germany, Italy, or Spain, or they can participate in an internship in Washington, DC.

Phillips Andover students have an equally interesting course catalog and student life. It's rare to find higher-level computer science classes at a high school, but Andover offers Data Structures and Algorithms, as well as Autonomous Systems. They offer an Economics Research Colloquium and Independent Projects, called IPs, which are for students who have exhausted the course offerings at the school. Andover students can apply for faculty-led spring break trips to interesting destinations around the world. Recent trips have included a ski trip across Finland, from the Russian border to the Swedish border; a Ghana adventure and cultural trip; Russian language immersion in Estonia; and, for the international students, a mini tour of the United States.

These are examples of offerings that are unique to selective boarding schools. There are many additional classes, activities, and opportunities that students will find at this type of school that they will not find locally.

WHAT TYPE OF STUDENT IS A GOOD MATCH FOR AN ULTRASELECTIVE SCHOOL?

Students who have already hit their stride academically, socially, and in extracurriculars are the strongest applicants for ultraselective schools. They should be able to show the admissions committee that they are ready to achieve academically, try new clubs or activities, and participate fully in school life.

When building your school application list, it is important to consider Admissions selectivity, as parents often mistakenly assume that certain schools are likely admits, when they are not. For example, they may know that Exeter and Andover are very selective but not realize that Blair has a low acceptance rate of only 14 percent. It's crucial to consider the likelihood of admission when building a school list. Parents should consider the schools listed in this category as a reach due to their selectivity rating for most applicants.

15

Single-Sex Boarding Schools

Many families who choose an all-boys or all-girls school don't necessarily set out to do so. They often consider a range of schools, both coed and single sex, and visit and research them fully. They may find themselves drawn to the campus culture and leadership opportunities at a single-sex school. Or they may choose the school based on reasons that don't have to do with it being an all-boys or all-girls school, such as its athletic or arts opportunities, distance from home, or simply a great experience at an on-campus visit. For parents who are skeptical about single-gender schools, I encourage you to investigate them fully before dismissing them, as they are often the root of a transformative high school experience.

GIRLS' SCHOOLS

Many of my clients tell me they would not consider a girls' school, and when they are pressed, I find it's often due to old stereotypes, misconceptions, or uncertainty about what the experience is like. At most girls' schools, there are plenty of opportunities to get to know boys through joint theater productions, trips, and social events. Some girls' schools coordinate so closely with local boys' schools that the students are as close as they would be if they went to school together. But if you ask any girl at a girls' school, she will tell you it isn't really about the boys anyway. They enjoy a daily life rooted in tradition, with class rings, big sisters, ceremonies, school songs, and joy. For many students at girls' schools, friendships grow deep and confidence is built; it's an experience they look back on fondly for life.

The benefits of all-girls education has been studied by the International Coalition of Girls' Schools. "Girls schools are places where girls take center stage. They occupy every seat in student government, every spot on the math team, and every position in the robotics club. In fact, *every* aspect of a girls' school—from the classroom to the athletic field to the academic program—is designed for girls. At their heart, girls' schools are places of leadership. Places where community and collaboration, agency and self-efficacy flourish. But most of all, girls' schools are places of incredible innovation."[1]

Girls who enjoy the teamwork and camaraderie of sports often enjoy the same all-girls environment in the classroom. "It just feels normal to me," says Katie, a student at Madeira. "I like my time with just girls. I was always on girls' sports teams, so this is like more of that type of bonding."

Anna, a student at Grier, said, "There's less drama at an all-girls school. The girls support each other. It also seems like girls are less focused on their appearance than they were at my old school."

A teacher at a girls' school said, "Everything here is for the girls. The turf field—it's for the girls. The community comes out to watch sporting events. Girls aren't seen as second best."

There are girls' schools with rigorous academic programs, strong STEM opportunities with engineering classes, and college placement at top colleges. There are also girls' schools that have nurturing and supportive academic programs where girls get the support they need to thrive in college.

Girls' boarding schools include Chatham Hall, Dana Hall, Emma Willard, Ethel Walker, Foxcroft, Garrison Forest, Grier, Linden Hall, Madeira, Miss Hall's, Miss Porter's, Santa Catalina, St. Margaret's, St. Timothy's, Saint Mary's, Stoneleigh-Burnham, and Westover.

BOYS' SCHOOLS

I worked with a boy who found not only a sense of confidence in himself after attending a boys' school but also the realization that he loved learning. He enthusiastically described classrooms where he worked in a team, competed, moved around a lot, and was encouraged to speak out. He spoke of male teachers, staff who appreciated boy humor, and people who "got him." He felt encouraged, and his teachers seemed like coaches who were rooting him on.

Students at boys' schools benefit from a culture that supports boys and the way they learn. They find a sense of camaraderie, and many become involved in the arts or activities they may not have felt comfortable joining in a coed school.

"I went to Salisbury for the sports," explained John, "but it ended up being one of those life-changing experiences. I was in the school play, something I never thought I would do. I made the best friends of my life. I learned how to study more efficiently and somehow it all came together and I got really good grades."

The International Boys School Coalition says,

> Boys and girls grow in different ways. MRIs demonstrate how boys' brains are wired to require movement, space, and rest. Learning more readily through action than words, boys may take longer to refine social, reading, and writing skills. Often more spatial and visual by nature, many boys demonstrate affinity for the abstract reasoning of math, science, and linguistics. Boys learn better when material is presented in small portions when they can connect learning to action, story, and outcome. Boys' schools create a learning environment premised on what

boys need. Educators at boys' school celebrate and value all that it means to be a boy.[2]

Boys' boarding schools include Avon Old Farms, Blue Ridge, Christ, Georgetown Prep, McCallie, Phelps, Salisbury, South Kent, Subiaco, Trinity Pawling, and Woodberry Forest.

Junior boarding boys' schools include Cardigan Mountain, Eaglebrook, Fessenden, Hillside, and St. Catherine's.

Boys' military schools include Army Navy, Camden, Fishburne, Fork Union, Hargrave, Missouri Military, Riverside Prep, Southern Prep, Marine Military, and Valley Forge.

16

Junior Boarding Schools

Junior boarding schools provide a caring environment with academic and extracurricular opportunities for middle school students. The staff at junior boarding schools are experts in working with this age group, and students benefit from living, working, and playing in a school community designed just for them.

Eaglebrook is a boys' school for grades 6–9 with a strong academic program and a busy and active daily life. The school has its own ski mountain, ice rink, and hundreds of acres for mountain biking and outdoor pursuits. Students can take an elective called Downhill Car Building, where they build a car that they can sit in and, ultimately, race against other students. Eaglebrook has a design lab, an engineering challenge, and a popular class called Tinkering With Circuits.

Cardigan Mountain is a boys' school for grades 6–9 with the core values of compassion, integrity, respect, and courage. You can see these values emphasized in the classroom, on the playing fields, and throughout the school community. Cardigan Mountain has traditions such as Mountain Day, when the whole school climbs a peak and has lunch at the top to best see the fall foliage, and the Sneaker Game, where boys work with a partner in a barefoot quest to find sneakers. Cardigan Mountain has a top ice hockey program, which has seen seven alumni make it to the NHL, and special programs for lacrosse and mountain biking.

Rectory is a K–9 coed school with boarders in grades 5–9; it offers a supportive community that includes an exceptional advisory program. "The purpose of the advisory program at Rectory is to be a second family," explains Dena Cocozza O'Hara, director of advisory. "It's the complete wrap-around care. Your child is known, cared for and nurtured here. And the advisor is your child's go-to person."[1] This close-knit relationship leads to happy students who are ready to achieve and take part in the school's many offerings, such as the May Experiential Learning Program, which is a "week-long excursion that uses the world as a classroom."[2]

These hand-on learning experiences include community service and have taken place in Puerto Rico, Charleston, and the great outdoors.

RECLASSING AT JUNIOR BOARDING SCHOOL

It's possible for students entering a junior boarding school to reclass, or repeat, a year of school. The extra year spent in the nurturing community of a junior boarding school, with the ability to take rigorous classes and get ready for high school, can be a game changer, both for getting into a selective school and for succeeding there.

While at his New York private school, Thomas, an eighth grader, didn't initially expect to reclass. He attended a boarding school summer camp and loved that experience, so he knew that boarding school, with its community feel and opportunities for sports and the outdoors, was for him. But as Thomas and his parents visited schools such as Exeter, Andover, and Choate, they noticed that the students seemed older than those in a typical high school. And with so many students entering Exeter, Andover, and Choate after ninth grade, as a reclassed student, or as a PG year student, the student body did indeed trend older than that in a typical high school. Thomas turned fourteen in June of eighth grade, so he was fairly young for his age. His parents felt that he would benefit from an extra year of growth and academic preparation before starting high school.

Thomas applied to Exeter, Andover, and Choate but also added Rumsey Hall, Fay, and Eaglebrook to his application list. He was accepted to all of the junior boarding schools but denied or wait-listed at the high schools. Thomas enrolled at Rumsey Hall as a reclassed eighth grader and immediately got involved by playing a sport each season and joining various clubs. His grades improved, and he learned to balance his schoolwork, activities, and social life. Thomas spent his eighth and ninth grade years at Rumsey Hall before enrolling at Choate as a tenth grader.

INTERNATIONAL STUDENTS AT JUNIOR BOARDING SCHOOL

Achieving English language fluency is easier at a young age, and junior boarding schools are the ultimate immersion experiences. Students from abroad are able to master the language and speak comfortably with other teens while also learning the ins and outs of life in an American school. When it comes to admission to selective high schools, international students who have proven their ability to succeed in a junior boarding school have an edge over their competitors.

Owen, a fifth grader from Shanghai, had parents who wanted him to have an American education. He was fortunate to have a US passport since he was born in Chicago while his parents were in graduate school. Owen's US citizenship meant that he would not need a visa to study in the United States, but he still faced difficult odds as a student applying from China for a limited number of spots in high school.

Owen's parents' jobs required them to travel frequently, and they felt that a junior boarding school located near his aunt and uncle in Boston would be ideal. He joined the sixth-grade class at Fessenden and stayed through eighth grade. Owen went on to Deerfield and credited his time at Fessenden as key in preparing him for high school success.

BOARDING SCHOOLS FOR GRADES 6–12

Although the term *junior boarding school* refers to schools that are focused on middle school boarding only, there are also a number of boarding schools that offer a combined middle and high school program, enrolling students in grades 6–12. Middle school enrollment is typically quite small at these schools, but it's a good option for parents who want small classes and the possibility of staying in the same school through high school graduation.

Schools with boarding offered in grades 6–12 include Brehm, Ethel Walker, IMG, MacDuffie, Perkiomen, Ross, Shattuck St. Mary's, among others. Some schools offer grades 8–12 enrollment, which offers students the opportunity to get used to the school academic program for a year, before the rigors of high school begin. Schools offering a grade 8–12 boarding enrollment include Eagle Hill, Garrison Forest, Groton, Grier, Saint James, St. Stephen's, Storm King, Trinity Pawling, Wilbraham and Monson, among others.

Junior boarding schools include the following:

- Applewild: coed boarding for grades 4–9
- Bement: coed boarding for grades 4–9
- Cardigan Mountain: boys boarding for grades 6–9
- Eaglebrook: boys boarding for grades 6–9
- Fay: coed boarding for grades 7–9
- Fessenden: boys boarding for grades 5–9
- Hillside: boys boarding for grades 4–9

Indian Mountain: coed boarding for grades 5–9
North Country: coed boarding for grades 4–9
Rectory: coed boarding for grades 5–9
Rumsey Hall: coed boarding for grades 5–9
St. Catherine's: boys boarding for grades 4–8

17

Military Schools

Today's military schools offer a modern educational environment that helps students succeed. Military schools are not treatment centers: they are not for bad kids, there is no hazing, and there is no commitment to join the military. Attending a military school is like going to any other boarding school, except with different rules and campus culture. The tuition at military schools is often significantly less than that of traditional boarding schools, and many parents are drawn to the value. Most military schools have both a middle school and high school program, and many are coed (with a smaller number of girls enrolled).

Hargrave Military Academy is a leading school whose students find academic and athletic success while also growing as individuals. Head of school and seasoned educator Eric Peterson is the former head of school at St. George's, which is a unique background for a military school head but one that has proven to be effective.

"We're not building soldiers," he explains. "It's not bootcamp, it's not a punishment, but the military environment provides the structure, consistency, and mechanism for leadership development. We put the boys first. Whatever they need drives our decision making."[1] It's clear this environment is bringing success to Hargrave students.

Parents today are concerned about their teens' use of screens and social media. It's common to see teens on their phones when they should be talking with peers or participating in activities. Hargrave has a stand-out policy in the boarding school world that has brought great success. They have phone-free weeks, meaning that the students' cell phones and iPads are placed in a locker on Sunday nights and returned to them on Fridays. They have access to their chrome books for schoolwork, but the fire wall blocks social media, ESPN, and other sites that attract the boys' attention. You won't see Hargrave boys on their phones or gaming during the week, but you will see them fishing, riding bikes, playing sports, and socializing with each other. The Hargrave campus has a paintball course, climbing tower, military obstacles course, an indoor pool, and athletic fields. "We're attentive to the emotional health and wellness of the students," Peterson explains. And the technology restrictions help them to do this. Very few cadets complain about phone-free week, as they are busy enjoying activities and socializing with friends.

Hargrave cadets can participate in the "Eye of the Tiger," which is "a multi-skilled, 20 hour long event over several days, designed to test each cadet's teamwork ability, physical and mental endurance, problem-solving skills, and grit, and is one of the toughest gut checks a young man will participate in."[2]

The Eye of the Tiger includes an obstacle course, fitness testing, a ruck march, night operations test, and water survival, among other things. Cadets graduate from Hargrave with the academic skills and confidence to achieve in college and beyond.

Cadets at Culver Military Academy start by learning the basics, including passing personal and room inspections; learning to manage their time appropriately; and learning to follow the lead of older students. As a member of the corps of cadets, each student joins either the infantry, artillery, the band, or the horseman squadron. By the time they graduate, many of the cadets can fire cannons, drive artillery trucks, or ride a horse with precision. And all can perform the proper customs and courtesies for parades and flag ceremonies. Culver has coed classes, with the boys participating in the military program and the girls attending a nonmilitary leadership program.

Admiral Farragut Academy is a United States Naval Honor School, accredited by the Department of the Navy. All students in grades 8 through 12 participate in the Naval Junior Reserve Officer Training Corps, which means that they wear a uniform, participate in drill and physical activities, and take naval science academic courses. All cadets learn to sail, and some learn to fly in the school's flight simulators or in planes at the local airport. Admiral Farragut makes good use of its waterfront location by making available marine science classes and scuba training and certification. Students applying to the US Naval Academy, US Air Force Academy, or the US Military Academy may have an admissions advantage since the school's Naval Honor School designation allows the school to nominate Admiral Farragut students so that they don't have to request a nomination from their local congressman.

Coed military schools include Admiral Farragut, Culver, Massanutten, New Mexico Military Institute, New York Military Academy, Oak Ridge, Randolph Macon, and St. John's Northwestern. Schools with an optional military program include TMI and San Marcos.

All-boys military schools include Army Navy, Camden, Fishburne, Fork Union, Hargrave, Marine Military, Missouri Military, Riverside Prep, Southern Prep, and Valley Forge. St Catherine's is a boarding military school for middle school boys.

18

Unique Boarding Schools

American boarding schools are more than just the typical coed school with a standard curriculum. Parents who want a high school experience for their children that is truly different from what is available at their local public or private school can find a variety of types of boarding schools. These schools get students excited about learning because of their different approaches to academics and daily life. Students who are bored with the typical grind of high school life may find something that excites them among these options.

United World College (https://www.uwc-usa.org/) is a school located in New Mexico for students in eleventh and twelfth grade that enrolls two hundred students from ninety different countries. Students can study for the prestigious International Baccalaureate diploma while living and learning with people from different cultures. It's part of a network of eighteen United World Colleges located throughout the world.

Their website states, "Students at UWC-USA start working to become agents for change the minute they set foot on campus. They build bridges to understanding with students of radically diverse nationalities, races, beliefs and economic backgrounds. They partner with a local homeless shelter, tutor children, and renovate a community center and learn to respect nature as they test their endurance in the wilderness. All while completing a rigorous IB diploma program at the same time. Our students learn lessons in practical idealism that equip them to become changemakers for life."[1]

Think Global School (www.thinkglobalschool.org) offers the educational journey of a lifetime. It is a traveling high school for fifty students in grades 10–12, who live and learn in four different countries each year. In 2025 the school is traveling to Botswana, India, Ecuador, and Greece, where students will study a rigorous curriculum while exploring the world around them through meaningful projects and interactions.

A+ World Academy (https://www.aplusworldacademy.com/) is a high school at sea. Sixty students travel with a maritime crew and teachers on a tall ship sailboat voyage. The school focuses on academics, global studies, community living, and developing maritime skills while students are seeing the world.

New England Innovation Academy (https://neiacademy.org/) is a one hundred-student boarding and day school outside of Boston with a goal "to prepare the next generation of innovators and entrepreneurs to pursue their dreams and shape a better world."[2] The Innovation Studio and entrepreneurship program are student favorites.

Princeton International School of Math and Science (PRISMS; https://prismsus.org/) is for students with a passion for STEM since PRISMS offers classes not often found in the typical high school, such as organic chemistry, engineering, linear algebra, and differential equations. A prominent feature of academic life there is the research and development program, where each student works on an independent or group project. The school offers a speaker series, with guests from the STEM world working with students. Founded and run by Chinese educators, Princeton International School of

Math and Science "is a school that merges the best educational philosophies from the East and the West."[3]

At the Mastery School of Hawken (https://masteryschool.hawken.edu/), a student's growth is at the center of everything they do, and the concept of mastery education allows for personal journeys and deep learning. Their website explains, "We use a methodology developed by our founding designer that helps you develop the deep and enduring skills needed for success in today's world: critical thinking, creative problem-solving, collaboration, communication, and citizenship. One way we do this is through Macros—interdisciplinary experiences where you work in teams for up to five hours a day to solve real challenges for a community partner. Macros include offerings in problem-solving, humanities, political systems, architecture, engineering, entrepreneurship, and more."[4] The Mastery School has 150 students, including 18 boarders, and is part of Hawken School's 650-student community.

HISTORICALLY BLACK BOARDING SCHOOLS

While there were once over one hundred historically Black boarding schools in the United States, now there are just four: Piney Woods in Mississippi, Pine Forge in Pennsylvania, Laurinburg Institute in South Carolina, and Redemption Christian Academy in New York. These schools provide more than just a college prep education; they are places for students to build connections, develop skills, and be part of a supportive community.

Taimya Adams, recent valedictorian of Piney Woods, described her time at the school: "I can be my authentic self. I can like what I want or do what I want. I can have whatever passion I want or speak a certain way." She continued, "I feel like I'm going to go out into the world knowing who I am, where I come from, and the history of my people in this country."[5]

Piney Woods has a 250-acre working farm on the 2,000-acre campus, and the students learn about farm work and entrepreneurship when they sell farmed products. William Crossley, the school's president, said, "The campus is our classroom, the land is our lab. Yesterday, we had students down on the farm caring for the animals. We've got eight horses, 60 to 65 head of cattle, roosters, chickens, goats, sheep and some farm dogs. There's something about caring for animals, and there's something about working with one's hands, that connects to one's brain."[6] The hard work on the farm and in the classroom leads to a 100 percent graduation rate and a strong record of college placement and successful alumni at Piney Woods.

EARLY COLLEGE

Highly motivated teens can start college right after tenth or eleventh grade. Bard College at Simon's Rock (https://simons-rock.edu/) "is real college, only sooner. It's not 'sort-of' college. [They] bring you face-to-face with big ideas, essential texts, deep and high-spirited discussion, advanced research, and the latest scholarship with professors who are tops in their fields."[7] The average new student is sixteen years old and joins a campus community of four hundred students from all over the world. Simon's Rock offers a rich extracurricular life including sports, the arts, and campus traditions.

Texas Academy of Mathematics and Science (https://tams.unt.edu/index.html) is an early college program on the campus of the University of North Texas. Top-performing high school students can apply for this residential program, which offers two years of college credits. Students enter one of six academic tracks: public health, math and science, computer science, engineering pathways, visual arts and design, or music.

ARTS AND ATHLETIC SPECIALTY SCHOOLS

As discussed in the chapter on athletics, there are schools that primarily focus on sports and the needs of young athletes. This includes tennis schools like Evert Tennis Academy, golf schools like the International Junior Golf Academy, and ski schools like Carrabassett Valley Academy.

IMG Academy is a sports training center that offers a boarding school program for athletes who hope to play in college and beyond. Students live in the dormitories and spend part of the day in school before training in their sport and participating in physical conditioning. Students come to IMG's boarding program to focus on basketball, baseball, football, golf, lacrosse, soccer, tennis, track and field, and volleyball. Spire Academy (www.spireacademy.com) is another sports-training boarding school that offers a boarding program and training for various sports.

Students who are passionate about the arts can attend one of the three arts boarding schools—Idyllwild, Interlochen, and Walnut Hill. These schools offer a strong academic curriculum along with study of visual arts, dance, theater, and media.

Admission to these specialized schools varies. Some will take almost any qualified student, while others have a selective admissions process. Parents interested in the specialized schools should talk to admissions representatives to gain insight on admissions requirements and the application process.

SCHOOLS WITH HIGH OR LOW BOARDING PERCENTAGES

It's important to consider the boarding-to-day-student ratio, as this can greatly influence your student's life at school. Schools in suburban areas often have a high percentage of day students, which can be ideal for those who want to be part of a large, vibrant school community located near shops and close to an airport or transportation center. Schools in rural areas tend to have a higher percentage of boarding students, meaning that weekend life is centered on campus and there are fewer students going home on weekends.

Culver, Episcopal, St. Paul's, and St. Andrew's of Delaware are 100 percent boarding schools, with no day students. This all-residential community means close connections with students and staff and an active weekend life on campus. The percentage of boarders at other schools varies. There are some schools with almost full boarding, at 90 percent, and others that have fewer than 10 percent boarding students.

Matthew, a ninth grader from Dallas, was looking for a school that had a strong football program, lots of school spirit, and an academic program that was challenging but supportive. Matthew's parents felt he was lost in his large public high school and that he would benefit from small classes, close interaction with teachers, and a place where he would be known and appreciated. They focused their search on schools in the New York suburban area since Matthew's father, John, worked in New York City one week per month and planned to visit his son frequently and watch some of his football games.

Matthew's family fell in love with the Hun School of Princeton. Located in a college town with plenty of shops and restaurants, it is only a short train ride to New York and close to the airport as well. Hun has 160 boarders, along with 480 day students. Matthew enrolled as a new sophomore and enjoyed being part of a close-knit boarding program. He played on the football team and tried lacrosse for the first time. He made friends with both boarders and day students and enjoyed monthly visits from his dad.

Julia was an eighth grader from Virginia who loved the beach and felt a connection to Florida from her times visiting her grandparents there. She considered local private schools but also investigated three boarding schools near the beach in Florida—Bolles, Admiral Farragut, and St. Andrew's. It was Julia driving the idea of boarding school, but her parents agreed to visit the schools and consider the options. The family was impressed with all three schools and noted the strong academic programs, extracurricular offerings, and happy student vibe. Julia had a great tour at St. Andrew's and connected with several teachers and students. The school is large, with over 1,100 students in grades K–12 but has just 100 boarders in the upper school. Julia liked the idea of a small boarding community within a larger school, enrolled in St. Andrew's, and instantly felt like she was a part of their welcoming community.

Schools with small boarding populations within a larger community include Athenian, Bolles, Brook Hill, Flintridge Sacred Heart, Georgetown Prep, Hun, Leman, Masters, Montverde, Oaks Christian, Pennington, St. Alban's, and Saint Andrew's of Florida, among others.

Many boarding schools offer five-day boarding programs, where the students go home on Fridays and return Sunday night. This allows students to avoid a commute to and from school during the week while getting family time at home on the weekends. Not all schools offer five-day boarding, since many have Saturday classes, sports, or other activities that would be difficult for the student to miss. There are a few schools that only offer five-day boarding, with all students returning home on Fridays. Schools that only offer boarding for five days include Belmont Hill, Nobles and Greenough, and Penguin Hall in Massachusetts; Hackley and Harvey in New York; and McDonough in Maryland.

BOARDING SCHOOLS ABROAD

Adventurous students can attend boarding school in various countries throughout the world. You can experience life in a traditional British boarding school, study Italian in Rome, ski and enjoy the mountain life in Switzerland, or explore the Middle East at a school in Jordan. Some students attend school overseas for only a year or semester to get a taste of life abroad, while others stay to graduate.

Chapter 18

Ashley, a tenth-grade student at a New Jersey public school, yearned for adventure and new experiences. She applied to St. Stephen's School in Rome (https://www.sssrome.it), an American school, and intended to spend the first semester of her junior year there. St. Stephen's offers a "year abroad" program where students can attend for one semester or one year before returning to their home school. Ashley found the adjustment overwhelming at first, as there was a lot to get used to, both from living in a new country and experiencing her first time living away from home. It took her some time to make friends with the Italian students, but once she did, she realized she was not ready to leave. She was invited home by day student friends, and she explored Rome and improved her Italian. Ashley decided to extend her semester abroad to a full year, and she happily finished her junior year at St. Stephen's.

Harrison was fascinated with international relations and had a personal goal of becoming the head of the Central Intelligence Agency (CIA) someday. He studied Arabic online and tried to learn about this important region. Harrison decided to spend his junior year at King's Academy in Jordan (https://www.kingsacademy.edu.jo/), a boarding school for students from all over the Middle East and the world. He was part of the Arabic Year program, where he studied Arabic and also learned about the history, politics, and culture of the region. Harrison got to know the families and communities of his friends in a way that was deeply meaningful to him. He finished his year at King's and felt like he understood the Middle East in a way that he never could have by studying the region at home.

Students interested in a semester or year abroad can attend a program with School Year Abroad (www.sya.org). Those interested in spending time in Switzerland can enroll at the famous Institut Le Rosey (https://www.rosey.ch/), which is one of the most expensive boarding schools in the world. They can also consider two American schools, Leysin (https://www.las.ch/) or TASIS, The American School in Switzerland (https://www.tasis.ch/), which has students from sixty countries. The Global College (https://theglobalcollege.com/) is a two-year International Baccalaureate program in Madrid that is open to students ages fifteen to eighteen from all over the world.

Students looking for a taste of life in the United Kingdom can consider EF Academy in Oxford (https://www.efacademy.org/en-us/) or TASIS England, The American School in England (https://www.tasisengland.org/). Boys can apply to Eton College (https://www.etoncollege.com/) and attend classes in buildings that are five hundred years old, wearing the traditional formal uniform of a black tailcoat with pinstripe pants, as well as a top hat on special occasions. St. Leonard's (https://www.stleonards-fife.org/) in Scotland is located in the world class golf town of St. Andrew's and offers a renowned golf academy program.

Canadian schools that are popular with American students include Brentwood College School (https://www.brentwood.ca/), Shawnigan Lake School (https://www.shawnigan.ca/), Bishop's College School (https://www.bishopscollegeschool.com/), and Stanstead College (https://www.stansteadcollege.com/).

SEMESTER SCHOOLS

Students who want a taste of boarding school life but don't want to be away from home for too long should consider a semester program. These are not traditional schools but, instead, are organizations that offer a specialized, semester-long program for sophomores or juniors. Students leave their home school for a semester, returning with academic credits and an enriched experience.

The Semester Schools Network (www.semesterschools.net) offers insight on their website, which says, "Students who attend our schools report advantages that go beyond their transcripts and college admissions results. Many of them report significant growth in less tangible areas, such as self-confidence, willingness to be a leader and ability to work well on a team. All of our schools are small communities, with no more than 35–60 students in each semester group. In addition, semester schools teach self-reliance through significant participation in making the community function."[8]

The School for Ethics and Global Leadership offers a program focused on ethical thinking skills, leadership development, and international relations in either London, Johannesburg, or Washington, DC. The Maine Coast Semester is a hands-on, experiential program that includes "backcountry adventures, science field labs, and daily opportunities to learn about sustainable living"[9] while students also take five academic classes. At the Island School in the Bahamas, semester students conduct research and learn about the environment but also participate in physical challenges, scuba diving, and community-engagement activities. Students at the Traveling School delve into communities in Africa or South America as they participate in field visits and community projects abroad. The US Senate Page School is a selective government program for eleventh graders to work on the Senate floor while attending school and living in Washington, DC.[10] Other semester schools include Alzar School, High Mountain Institute, Mountain School, and the Outdoor Academy.

Appendix
Directory of Boarding Schools by State

This list includes many of the boarding schools in the United States; however, it doesn't include all of the boarding options available. There are many smaller schools, unaccredited schools, and schools with homestay programs that have not been included in this list.

Alabama

Indian Springs School (https://www.indiansprings.org/)
Southern Prep Academy (https://southernprepacademy.org/)
St. Bernard Prep School (https://stbernardprep.com)

Arizona

Orme School (https://www.ormeschool.org/)
Rancho Solano Prep (https://ranchosolano.com/)
Valley Verde School (https://www.vvsaz.org/)

Arkansas

Subiaco Academy (https://www.subiacoacademy.us/)

California

Army and Navy Academy (https://www.armyandnavyacademy.org/)
Athenian School (https://www.athenian.org/)
Besant Hill School (https://www.besanthill.org/)
Cate School (https://www.cate.org/)
Dunn School (https://www.dunnschool.org/)
EF Academy (https://www.efacademy.org/en-us/pasadena/)
Flintridge Sacred Heart (https://www.fsha.org/)
Idyllwild Arts Academy (https://idyllwildarts.org/)
Lake Tahoe Prep (https://laketahoeprep.org/)
Midland School (https://midland-school.org/)
Oaks Christian (https://www.oakschristian.org/)
Ojai Valley School (https://www.ovs.org/)
San Domenico School (https://www.ovs.org/)
Santa Catalina School (https://www.santacatalina.org/)
Sierra Canyon School (https://www.sierracanyonschool.org/)
Southwestern Academy (https://southwesternacademy.edu)
St. Catherine's Academy (https://www.stcatherinesacademy.org/)
Stevenson School (https://stevensonschool.org/)
Thacher School (https://www.thacher.org/)
Villanova Preparatory School (https://www.villanovaprep.org/)
The Webb Schools (https://www.webb.org/)
Woodside Priory School (https://www.prioryca.org/)

Colorado

Colorado Rocky Mountain School (https://www.crms.org/)
Eagle Rock School (https://www.eaglerockschool.org/)
Fountain Valley School (https://www.fvs.edu/)
Steamboat Mountain School (https://steamboatmountainschool.org/)

Connecticut

Avon Old Farms School (https://www.avonoldfarms.com/)
Canterbury School (https://www.cbury.org/)

Cheshire Academy (https://cheshireacademy.org/)
Choate Rosemary Hall School (https://www.choate.edu/)
Ethel Walker School (https://www.ethelwalker.org/)
Forman School (https://www.formanschool.org/)
Franklin Academy (https://fa-ct.org/)
Frederick Gunn School (https://www.frederickgunn.org/)
Glenholme School (https://theglenholmeschool.org/)
Grove School (https://www.groveschool.org/)
Hotchkiss School (https://www.hotchkiss.org/)
Indian Mountain School (https://www.indianmountain.org/)
Kent School (https://www.kent-school.edu/)
Loomis Chaffee School (https://www.loomischaffee.org/)
Marianapolis Prep School (https://www.marianapolis.org/)
Marvelwood School (https://www.marvelwood.org/)
Miss Porter's School (https://www.porters.org/)
Oxford Academy (https://oxfordacademy.net/)
Pomfret School (https://www.pomfret.org/)
Rectory School (https://www.rectoryschool.org/)
Rumsey Hall School (https://www.rumseyhall.org/)
Salisbury School (https://www.salisburyschool.org/)
South Kent School (https://southkentschool.org/)
St. Thomas More School (https://stmct.org/)
Suffield Academy (https://www.suffieldacademy.org/)
Taft School (https://www.taftschool.org/)
Westminster School (https://www.westminster-school.org/)
Westover School (https://www.westoverschool.org/)
Woodhall School (https://woodhallschool.org/)
Woodstock Academy (www.woodstockacademy.org)

Delaware

St. Andrew's School (https://www.standrews-de.org/)

District of Columbia

St. Alban's School (https://www.stalbansschool.org/)

Florida

Admiral Farragut Academy (https://farragut.org/)
Bolles School (https://www.bolles.org/)
Florida Prep Academy (https://www.flprep.com/)
IMG Academy (https://www.imgacademy.com/)
Montverde Academy (https://montverde.org/)
North Broward Prep School (https://www.nordangliaeducation.com/)
Saint Andrew's School (https://www.saintandrews.net/)
Vanguard School (https://www.vanguardschool.org/)

Georgia

Darlington School (https://www.darlingtonschool.org/)
Rabun Gap-Nacoochee School (https://www.rabungap.org/)
Riverside Prep School (https://www.riversideprep.org/)
Tallulah Falls School (https://www.tallulahfalls.org/)

Hawaii

Hawaii Prep Academy (https://www.hpa.edu/)
Iolani School (https://www.iolani.org/)

Idaho

Riverstone International School (https://www.riverstoneschool.org/)
Sun Valley Community School (https://www.communityschool.org/)

Illinois

Brehm Prep School (https://www.brehm.org/)
Lake Forest Academy (https://www.lfanet.org/)
St. Bede Academy (https://www.st-bede.com/)
Woodlands Academy (https://www.woodlandsacademy.org/)

Indiana

Culver Academies (https://www.culver.org/)
La Lumiere School (https://www.lalumiere.org/)

Kansas

Maur Hill-Mount Academy (https://mh-ma.com/)

Maine

Bridgton Academy (https://bridgtonacademy.org/)
Carrabassett Valley Academy (https://www.gocva.com/)
Fryeburg Academy (https://www.fryeburgacademy.org/)
Gould Academy (https://www.gouldacademy.org/)
Hebron Academy (https://www.hebronacademy.org/)
Hyde School (https://www.hyde.edu/)
Kents Hill School (https://www.kentshill.org/)
Washington Academy (https://www.washingtonacademy.org/)

Maryland

Boys' Latin School (https://www.boyslatinmd.com/)
Garrison Forest School (https://www.gfs.org/)
Georgetown Prep School (https://www.gprep.org/)
Saint James School (https://www.stjames.edu/)
Sandy Spring Friends School (https://www.ssfs.org/)
St. Timothy's School (https://www.stt.org/)
West Nottingham School (https://wna.org/)

Massachusetts

Applewild School (https://www.applewild.org/)
Bard Academy of Simon's Rock (https://bardacademy.simons-rock.edu/)
Bement School (https://www.bement.org/)
Berkshire School (https://www.berkshireschool.org/)

Brooks School (https://www.brooksschool.org/)
Buxton School (https://buxtonschool.org/)
Cambridge School of Weston (https://www.csw.org/)
Chapel Hill–Chauncy Hall (https://www.chch.org/)
Concord Academy (https://concordacademy.org/)
Cushing Academy (https://www.cushing.org/)
Dana Hall School (https://www.danahall.org/)
Eaglebrook School (https://www.eaglebrook.org/)
Eagle Hill School (https://www.eaglehill.school/)
Fay School (https://www.fayschool.org/)
Fessenden School (https://www.fessenden.org/)
Governor's Academy (https://www.thegovernorsacademy.org/)
Groton School (https://www.groton.org/)
Hillside School (https://www.hillsideschool.net/)
Landmark School (https://www.landmarkschool.org/)
Lawrence Academy (https://www.lacademy.edu/)
Lexington Christian (https://lca.edu/)
MacDuffie School (https://macduffie.org/)
Milton Academy (https://www.milton.edu/)
Miss Hall's School (https://www.misshalls.org/)
Newman School (https://www.newmanboston.org/)
Northfield Mt. Hermon (https://www.nmhschool.org/)
Phillips Academy Andover (https://www.andover.edu/)
Riverview School (https://www.riverviewschool.org/)
St. Mark's School (https://www.stmarksschool.org/)
Stoneleigh-Burnham School (https://sbschool.org/)
Tabor Academy (https://www.taboracademy.org/)
Walnut Hill School for the Arts (https://www.walnuthillarts.org/)
Wilbraham and Monson Academy (https://www.wma.us/)
Williston Northampton School (https://www.williston.com/)
Winchendon School (https://winchendon.org/)
Worcester Academy (https://www.worcesteracademy.org/)

Michigan

Cranbrook School (https://schools.cranbrook.edu/)
Interlochen Arts Academy (https://www.interlochen.org/)
Leelanau School (https://leelanau.org/)
Michigan Lutheran (https://michiganlutheran.org/)

Minnesota

Cotter School (https://www.cotterschools.org/)
International School of Minnesota (https://international schoolmn.com/)
Shattuck-St. Mary's School (https://www.s-sm.org/)
St. Croix Lutheran Academy (https://www.stcroixlutheran.org/)
St. John's Prep (https://sjprep.net/)

Mississippi

Piney Woods School (https://www.pineywoods.org/)
St. Stanislaus School (https://ststan.com/)

Missouri

Chaminade College Prep (https://www.chaminade-stl.org/)
Missouri Military Academy (https://www.missourimilitaryacademy.org/)
St. Paul Lutheran (https://splhs.org/)
Thomas Jefferson School (https://www.tjs.org/)

New Hampshire

Brewster Academy (https://www.brewsteracademy.org/)
Cardigan Mountain School (https://www.cardigan.org/)
Dublin School (https://www.dublinschool.org/)
Gould Academy (https://www.gouldacademy.org/)

Hampshire Country School (https://www.hampshirecountryschool.org/)
High Mowing School (https://www.highmowing.org/)
Holderness School (https://www.holderness.org/)
Kimball Union Academy (https://www.kua.org/)
New Hampton School (https://www.newhampton.org/)
Oliverian School (https://www.oliverianschool.org/)
Phillips Exeter Academy (https://exeter.edu/)
Proctor Academy (https://www.proctoracademy.org/)
St. Paul's School (https://www.sps.edu/)
Tilton School (https://tiltonschool.org/)

New Jersey

Blair Academy (https://www.blair.edu/)
Hun School of Princeton (https://www.hunschool.org/)
Lawrenceville School (https://www.lawrenceville.org/)
Peddie School (https://peddie.org/)
Pennington School (https://www.pennington.org/)

New Mexico

New Mexico Military Institute (https://www.nmmi.edu/)

New York

Buffalo Seminary (https://www.buffaloseminary.org/)
Darrow School (https://www.darrowschool.org/)
EF Academy (https://www.efacademy.org/en-us/new-york/)
Emma Willard School (https://www.emmawillard.org/)
Gow School (https://www.gow.org/)
Hoosac School (https://hoosac.org/)
Knox School (https://www.knoxschool.org/)
Leman Manhattan (https://www.lemanmanhattan.org/)
Maplebrook School (https://www.maplebrookschool.org/)
The Masters School (https://www.mastersny.org/)
Millbrook School (https://www.millbrook.org/)

Directory of Boarding Schools by State

New York Military Academy (https://www.nyma.org/)
North Country School (https://northcountryschool.org/)
Northwood School (https://northwoodschool.org/)
Oakwood Friends School (https://www.oakwoodfriends.org/)
Redemption Christian Academy (https://redemptionchristianacademy.org/)
Ross School (https://www.ross.org/)
The Stony Brook School (https://www.sbs.org/)
Storm King School (https://sks.org/)
Trinity Pawling School (https://www.trinitypawling.org/)

North Carolina

Asheville School (https://www.ashevilleschool.org/)
Christ School (https://www.christschool.org/)
Laurinburg Institute (https://www.laurinburginstitute.org/)
Oak Ridge Military Academy (https://www.oakridgemilitary.com/)
Salem Academy (https://salemacademy.com/)
St. Mary's Academy (https://www.sms.edu/)

Ohio

Andrews Osborne Academy (https://www.andrewsosborne.org/)
Gilmour Academy (https://www.gilmour.org/)
Grand River Academy (https://www.grandriver.org/)
Western Reserve Academy (https://www.wra.net/)

Oregon

Delphian School (https://www.delphian.org/)
Oregon Episcopal School (https://www.oes.edu/)

Pennsylvania

Church Farm School (https://www.gocfs.net/)
George School (https://www.georgeschool.org/)
Grier School (https://www.grier.org/)
Hill School (https://www.thehill.org/)
Linden Hall School (https://www.lindenhall.org/)
Kiski School (https://www.kiski.org/)
Mercersburg Academy (https://www.mercersburg.edu/)
Milton Hershey School (https://www.mhskids.org/)
Perkiomen School (https://www.perkiomen.org/)
Phelps School (https://www.thephelpsschool.org/)
Pine Forge Academy (https://www.pineforgeacademy.org/)
Shady Side Academy (https://www.shadysideacademy.org/)
Solebury School (https://www.solebury.org/)
Valley Forge Military Academy (https://www.vfmac.edu/)
Westtown School (https://www.westtown.edu/)
Wyoming Seminary (https://www.wyomingseminary.org/)

Rhode Island

Middlebridge School (https://www.middlebridgeschool.org/)
Portsmouth Abbey School (https://www.portsmouthabbey.org/)
St. Andrew's School (https://www.standrews-ri.org/)
St. George's School (https://www.stgeorges.edu/)

South Carolina

Camden Military Academy (https://camdenmilitary.com/)
Hilton Head Prep (https://www.hhprep.org/)

Tennessee

Baylor School (https://www.baylorschool.org/)
Currey Ingram Academy (https://www.curreyingram.org/)

McCallie School (https://www.mccallie.org/)
St. Andrew's-Sewanee School (https://www.sasweb.org/)
The Webb School (https://www.thewebbschool.com/)

Texas

Brook Hill School (https://www.brookhill.org/)
Marine Military Academy (https://www.mma-tx.org/)
San Marcos Academy (https://www.smabears.org/)
St. Stephen's Episcopal School (https://www.sstx.org/)
TMI Episcopal School (https://www.tmi-sa.org/)

Utah

Wasatch Academy (https://www.wasatchacademy.org/)

Vermont

Burke Mountain School (https://www.burkemtnacademy.org/)
Greenwood School (https://greenwood.org/)
Lyndon Institute (https://www.lyndoninstitute.org/)
Putney School (https://www.putneyschool.org)
Rock Point School (https://www.rockpointschool.org/)
St. Johnsbury Academy (https://stjacademy.org/)
Stratton Mountain School (https://www.gosms.org/)
Vermont Academy (https://www.vermontacademy.org/)

Virginia

Blue Ridge School (https://www.blueridgeschool.com/)
Chatham Hall School (https://www.chathamhall.org/)
Christchurch School (https://www.christchurchschool.org/)
Episcopal High School (https://www.episcopalhighschool.org/)
Fishburne Military School (https://www.fishburne.org/)
Fork Union Military Academy (https://www.forkunion.com/)
Foxcroft School (https://www.foxcroft.org/)

Hargrave Military Academy (https://hargrave.edu/)
Madeira School (https://www.madeira.org/)
Massanutten Military Academy (https://www.militaryschool.com/)
Miller School of Albemarle (https://millerschoolofalbemarle.org/)
North Cross School (https://www.northcross.org/)
Oak Hill Academy (https://oak-hill.net/)
Randolph Macon Academy (https://rma.edu/)
St. Anne's Belfield School (https://www.stab.org/)
St. Margaret's School (https://www.sms.org/)
Stuart Hall School (https://www.stuarthallschool.org/)
Virginia Episcopal School (https://www.ves.org/)
Woodberry Forest School (https://www.woodberry.org/)

Washington

Annie Wright Schools (https://www.aw.org/)
The Northwest School (https://www.northwestschool.org/)

West Virginia

Linsly School (https://www.linsly.org/)

Wisconsin

St. John's Northwestern Academy (https://sjnacademies.org/)
St. Lawrence Seminary High School (https://www.stlawrence.edu/)
Wayland Academy (https://www.wayland.org/)
Wisconsin Lutheran (https://www.wlhs.org/)

Notes

CHAPTER 2

1. Raj Chetty, David Deming, and John N. Friedman, "Diversifying Society's Leaders? The Determinants and Consequences of Admission to Highly Selective Colleges," *Opportunity Insights*, October 2023, https://opportunityinsights.org/wp-content/uploads/2023/07/CollegeAdmissions_Nontech.pdf.
2. https://admissionbydesign.com/wp-content/uploads/2021/08/Teacher-Evaluation-Form-Common-Application.pdf.
3. Jim Jump, "Ethical College Admissions: The College Counselor as Hollywood Agent," *Inside Higher Ed*, September 6, 2021, https://www.insidehighered.com/admissions/views/2021/09/07/high-school-counselors-dont-have-real-influence-opinion.
4. Chetty, Deming, and Friedman, "Diversifying Society's Leaders?"

CHAPTER 5

1. Andrew Gagnon, letter to Andover parents, March 2023, Phillips Academy, https://www.andover.edu/files/ADM/TF2023-24.pdf.

2. Salisbury School, "Tuition & Fees," accessed October 2024, https://www.salisburyschool.org/become-a-knight/tuition-fees.

3. Western Reserve Academy, "Space and Poetry Inspire New Full Tuition Scholarship," accessed October 2024, https://www.wra.net/news/2023-10-09/space-and-poetry-inspire-new-full-tuition-scholarship.

4. Institute for Educational Advancement, "IEA's Caroline D. Bradley Scholarship Offers One of the Only Merit-Based, Need-Blind High School Scholarships to Highly Gifted Students across the United States," last updated 2024, https://educationaladvancement.org/caroline-d-bradley-scholarship/.

CHAPTER 6

1. Ryan Mulhern, phone interview with author, April 24, 2024.

2. South Kent School, "Admissions FAQ," accessed October 2024, https://southkentschool.org/admissions-faqs/.

3. https://www.blair.edu/about-blair/publications-news/post/~board/news/post/state-of-admission.

CHAPTER 8

1. Peddie, "About Peddie," The Peddie School, last updated 2024, https://www.peddie.org/about/.

2. Sophie Zhu, "History of Surprise Holiday," *The Circle Voice*, March 2, 2024, https://thecirclevoice.org/6752/features/history-of-surprise-holiday/.

3. Deerfield, "Family Dinner at Deerfield," Deerfield Academy, posted November 6, 2019, https://deerfield.edu/parents/news/family-dinner-at-deerfield/3757.

4. Deerfield, "Family Dinner at Deerfield."

5. Deerfield, "Family Dinner at Deerfield."

6. Northfield Mount Hermon, "Workjob," last updated 2022, https://www.nmhschool.org/campus-life/workjob.

7. Holderness, "Job Program," accessed October 2024, https://www.holderness.org/student-life/leadership-service.

8. https://www.proctoracademy.org/athletics/afternoon-activities.

9. https://www.proctoracademy.org/athletics/afternoon-activities.

CHAPTER 9

1. Jon Posner, phone interview with author, May 2024.
2. Peter Verhoef, email interview with author, May 2024.
3. Christa Talbot-Syfu, email interview with author, May 2024.
4. Shattuck-St. Mary's School, "Golf Center of Excellence," accessed October 2024, https://www.s-sm.org/athletics/golf-center-of-excellence.
5. Kevin Czepiel, email interview with author.

CHAPTER 10

1. St. Paul's School, "Dance," last updated 2023, https://www.sps.edu/arts/dance.
2. IMDb, "Dominic Sessa Awards," last updated 2024, https://www.imdb.com/name/nm14073757/awards/.
3. Svetlana Deshpande, "Artist of the Issue: Dominic Sessa," *Deerfield Scroll*, June 2, 2022, https://deerfieldscroll.com/2022/06/artist-of-the-issue-dominic-sessa/.
4. https://www.interlochen.org/arts-boarding-school.

CHAPTER 11

1. Leah Mason and Natalya Andrejko, *Studying for the Future: International Students in the United States* (New York: Institute of International Education, 2020), https://iie.widen.net/s/r2trwgnvbq.
2. Thomas Yu, "What Is the Gaokao? A Look at China's Daunting Entrance Exams," *South China Morning Post*, June 7, 2024.
3. Caralyn Dea, email interview with author, April 2024.
4. Metta Dael, email interview with author, April 2024.

CHAPTER 12

1. Forman, "Application Process," Forman School, accessed October 2024, https://www.formanschool.org/admissions/apply.
2. From https://www.frederickgunn.org/academics/academic-support/learning-support.

3. Kents Hill School, "Academic Support," accessed October 2024, https://www.kentshill.org/academics/academic-support.

4. Trinity-Pawling School, "Center for Learning Achievement," last updated 2021, https://www.trinitypawling.org/academics/center-for-learning-achievement.

5. Little Elf, "Our Story," Little Elf Products, Inc., last updated 2024, https://www.littleelfproducts.com/pages/our-story?srsltid=AfmBOoqQMV4uFatD1g_ShKPXLNCMEF1sJoWdehRdjQXjvK21GDu7u7M2.

6. https://www.eaglehill.school/admission/frequently-asked-questions.

7. Landmark School, "Landmark Approach," last updated 2024, https://www.landmarkschool.org/our-advantage/landmark-approach.

8. Matt Woodhall, email interview with author, May 2024.

9. Hampshire Country School, "HCS Mission," last updated 2024, https://www.hampshirecountryschool.org/discover-hcs/mission.

10. Krissy Naspo, email interview with author, May 2024.

CHAPTER 14

1. Ten Schools Admission Organization, "TSAO Member Schools," Ten Schools, accessed October 2024, https://www.tenschools.org.

2. Murex Robotics, "Welcome to mrxEE," Murex, last updated 2024, https://www.murexrobotics.com/mrxEE/.

CHAPTER 15

1. International Coalition of Girls' Schools, "Why Girls' Schools," ICGS, accessed October 2024, https://girlsschools.org/advocacy/why-girls-schools/.

2. International Boys' Schools Coalition, "Boys' Schools Understand and Celebrate Boys," IBSC, accessed October 2024, https://www.theibsc.org/about-ibsc/celebrate.

CHAPTER 16

1. https://www.rectoryschool.org/academics/middle-school-5-9-academics/beyond-academics.
2. Rectory School, "May Experiential Learning Program (MELP)," last updated 2020, https://www.rectoryschool.org/academics/middle-school-5-9-academics/melp.

CHAPTER 17

1. Eric Peterson, phone interview with author, March 2024.
2. Nick Morris, "Eye of the Tiger," Hargrave, Be More, published March 12, 2019, https://hargrave.edu/news/eye-of-the-tiger-2019/.

CHAPTER 18

1. UWC-USA, "About Us," last updated 2024, https://www.uwc-usa.org/about-us/.
2. www.neiacademy.org.
3. Pengzhi Liu, "About," PRISMS, last updated 2024, https://prismsus.org/about/#mission.
4. Mastery School of Hawken, "Our Approach to Education," last updated 2023, https://masteryschool.hawken.edu/about-msh.
5. Danielle Prescod, "The Last Black Boarding School," *Elle*, June 19, 2024, https://www.elle.com/culture/career-politics/a61146049/piney-woods-boarding-school-legacy/.
6. Sierra Lyons, "Before 'Brown,' the U.S. Had 100 Black Boarding Schools. Now, There Are 4," *The 74*, May 16, 2024, https://www.the74million.org/article/before-brown-the-u-s-had-100-black-boarding-schools-now-there-are-4/.
7. Bard College at Simon's Rock, "Real College, Only Sooner," last updated 2024, https://simons-rock.edu/early-college/index.php.
8. Semester Schools Network, "Why a Semester School?," last updated 2024, https://semesterschools.net/why-a-semester-school/.
9. https://mainecoastsemester.chewonki.org/.
10. United States Senate Page School, "U.S. Senate Page Program," accessed October 2024, https://pageprogram.senate.gov/.

Bibliography

Chetty, Raj, David Deming, and John M. Friedman. "Diversifying Society's Leaders? The Determinants and Consequences of Admission to Highly Selective Colleges." *Opportunity Insights*, October 2023. https://opportunityinsights.org/wp-content/uploads/2023/07/CollegeAdmissions_Nontech.pdf.

Deerfield. "Deerfield Academy." Last updated 2023. https://deerfield.edu/.

Deshpande, Svetlana. "Artist of the Issue: Dominic Sessa." *Deerfield Scroll*, June 2, 2022. https://deerfieldscroll.com/2022/06/artist-of-the-issue-dominic-sessa/.

Forman. "Application Process." Forman School. Accessed October 2024. https://www.formanschool.org/admissions/apply.

Gagnon, Andrew. Letter to Andover parents, March 2023, Phillips Academy. https://www.andover.edu/files/ADM/TF2023-24.pdf.

Hampshire Country School. "HCS Mission." Last updated 2024. https://www.hampshirecountryschool.org/discover-hcs/mission.

Holderness. "Job Program." Accessed October 2024. https://www.holderness.org/student-life/leadership-service.

IMDb. "Dominic Sessa Awards." Last updated 2024. https://www.imdb.com/name/nm14073757/awards/.

Institute for Educational Advancement. "IEA's Caroline D. Bradley Scholarship Offers One of the Only Merit-Based, Need-Blind High School Scholarships to Highly Gifted Students across the United States." Last updated 2024. https://educationaladvancement.org/caroline-d-bradley-scholarship/.

International Boys' Schools Coalition. "Boys' Schools Understand and Celebrate Boys." IBSC. Accessed October 2024. https://www.theibsc.org/about-ibsc/celebrate.

International Coalition of Girls' Schools. "Why Girls' Schools." ICGS. Accessed October 2024. https://girlsschools.org/advocacy/why-girls-schools/.

Jump, Jim. "Ethical College Admissions: The College Counselor as Hollywood Agent." *Inside Higher Ed*, September 6, 2021. https://www.insidehighered.com/admissions/views/2021/09/07/high-school-counselors-dont-have-real-influence-opinion.

Kents Hill School. "Academic Support." Accessed October 2024. https://www.kentshill.org/academics/academic-support.

Landmark School. "Landmark Approach." Last updated 2024. https://www.landmarkschool.org/our-advantage/landmark-approach.

Little ELF. "Our Story." Little ELF Products, Inc. Last updated 2024. https://www.littleelfproducts.com/pages/our-story?srsltid=AfmBOoqq3QE4J3s2yXcysnWdqT42d_FK0oSmcLPeOAKoWqXv-LIpUXkpE.

Liu, Pengzhi. "About." PRISMS. Last updated 2024. https://prismsus.org/about/#mission.

Lyons, Sierra. "Before 'Brown,' the U.S. Had 100 Black Boarding Schools. Now, There Are 4." *The 74*, May 16, 2024. https://www.the74million.org/article/before-brown-the-u-s-had-100-black-boarding-schools-now-there-are-4/.

Mason, Leah, and Natalya Andrejko. *Studying for the Future: International Students in the United States*. New York: Institute of International Education, 2020. https://iie.widen.net/s/r2trwgnvbq.

Mastery School of Hawken. "Our Approach to Education." Last updated 2023. https://masteryschool.hawken.edu/about-msh.

Morris, Nick. "Eye of the Tiger." Hargrave, Be More. Published March 12, 2019. https://hargrave.edu/news/eye-of-the-tiger-2019/.

Murex Robotics. "Welcome to mrxEE." Murex. Last updated 2024. https://www.murexrobotics.com/mrxEE/.

Northfield Mount Hermon. "Workjob." Last updated 2022. https://www.nmhschool.org/campus-life/workjob.

Peddie. "About Peddie." The Peddie School. Last updated 2024. https://www.peddie.org/about/.

Prescod, Danielle. "The Last Black Boarding School." *Elle*, June 19, 2024. https://www.elle.com/culture/career-politics/a61146049/piney-woods-boarding-school-legacy/.

Rectory School. "May Experiential Learning Program (MELP)." Last updated 2020. https://www.rectoryschool.org/academics/middle-school-5-9-academics/melp.

Salisbury School. "Tuition & Fees." Accessed October 2024. https://www.salisburyschool.org/become-a-knight/tuition-fees.

Semester Schools Network. "Why a Semester School?" Last updated 2024. https://semesterschools.net/why-a-semester-school/.

South Kent School. "Admissions FAQ." Accessed October 2024. https://southkentschool.org/admissions-faqs/.

St. Paul's School. "Dance." Last updated 2023. https://www.sps.edu/arts/dance.

Ten Schools Admission Organization. "TSAO Member Schools." Ten Schools. Accessed October 2024. https://www.tenschools.org.

Trinity-Pawling School. "Center for Learning Achievement." Last updated 2021. https://www.trinitypawling.org/academics/center-for-learning-achievement.

United States Senate Page School. "U.S. Senate Page Program." Accessed October 2024. https://pageprogram.senate.gov/.

UWC-USA. "About Us." Last updated 2024. https://www.uwc-usa.org/about-us/.

Western Reserve Academy. "Space and Poetry Inspire New Full Tuition Scholarship." Accessed October 2024. https://www.wra.net/news/2023-10-09/space-and-poetry-inspire-new-full-tuition-scholarship.

Yu, Thomas. "What Is the Gaokao? A Look at China's Daunting Entrance Exams." *South China Morning Post*, June 7, 2024.

Zhu, Sophie. "History of Surprise Holiday." *The Circle Voice*, March 2, 2024. https://thecirclevoice.org/6752/features/history-of-surprise-holiday/.

Index

Page numbers in italics refer to table.

academics, 5; at all-girls' schools, 176–77; evaluating, 83; learning support programs, 21, 86, 150–53; nonacademic credentials, 29
access programs, 65
ACT, 26, 50
ADHD, 5, 21, 86; high IQ along with, 155–56; learning-support schools and, 153–55; tests for determining, 51
Admiral Farragut Academy, 187
admissions, boarding school, 11; athletes in process of, 112–15; decision notification, 81–82; demographics factor, 69; denied, 15; enrollment decision deadline, 81–82; for international students, 138–39; interview feedback from, 41–42; interview questions asked by directors of, 41; letters and advocacy calls with directors, 72–74; mailing list, 43–44; PG year, 164; professional help with, 14; representatives, 13; selective schools and international, 140–41; selectivity, 15–16; wait list, 74–76. *See also* college admissions
admissions committees: applicant characteristics sought by, 67–69; artists sought by, 129–30; concept, 67; discussions, 69–72; international student evaluation by, 142–43
advocacy calls, 72–74
age, of entry, 8–9
alcohol usage, 83–84, 87, 90
All Kinds of Therapy, 158

221

American School in England, 197
Andover, 56–62, 78, 132, 147, 166, 173; computer science classes, 172; Exeter and, 17, 101; ice hockey and, 110, 111, 121; lacrosse games, 122; sports competitions and, 102; sports programs, 121, 122, 126
annual tuition, 55–57
A+ World Academy, 190
Applewild, 182
applications and application process: the arts and, 129–30; case studies, 76–79; from China, 142; choice between two, 44; "common," 44; communication during, 42; decision notification, 81–82; financial aid, 58–59; frequently asked questions about, 51–53; graded essays and, 47–48; inquiry form, 43–44; interview as part of, 33; parent essays, 46; period, 11; recommendations, 48–49, 68, 71; reply date, 76; student essays, 45–46; testing, 49–51; test prep, 51; video and multimedia submissions, 46–47; when to start researching and applying, 11
Army and Navy Academy, 56, 178, 187
arts, 192; application process and, 129–30; boarding schools focused on, 135; facilities, 129; opportunities for sports and, 5–6; schools celebrating, 131; specialty schools, 193; visual, 130–31
Asheville, 56, 118
Association of Boarding Schools, 13
athletes, 29, 75; in admissions process, 112–15; elite, 109–11; PG year and, 161–64; reclassing and, 110; sports for all levels of, 107
athletics: boarding school view of, 107; coaches, 32; elite athletes and, 109–11; evaluating programs in, 115–16; finding new sport, 107–9; selected school programs for, 116–27; specialty schools, 193; training, 56
Avon Old Farms, 62, 166, 178; football, 119; ice hockey, 121; weekend fun, 96–97

Babson College, 25
Bard College, 192
baseball, 163–64
basketball, 116–18, 163
Baylor, 56, 62, 119, 125–26; golf dynasty, 120
Bement, 182
Berkshire School, 100, 121, 166
A Better Chance, 14, 65
Blair Academy, 69, 118, 163, 166; acceptance rate, 173
Blue Ridge, 178
boarding school life. *See* daily life, at boarding school
Boarding School Review, 13
boarding schools: abroad, 195–97; applications to multiple, 44–45; building list of, 15–16; Chinese family example, 7–8; choosing after acceptance, 82–83; common age and grade for entering, 8–9; comparing, 83; free, 63–64; for grades 6-12, 182–83; with high or low boarding percentages, 193–95; historically Black, 191–92; involuntarily leaving, 87–89; junior, 182–83; lease expensive, 56; list of all-boys', 178; list of all-girls', 177; low-priced, 63; most recognized, 56; overview of PG, 166;

Index

problems at, 83–84; reasons for choosing, 3–7; reasons for leaving, 87; separation aspect, 7–8; therapeutic, 157–58; unique, 189–91; voluntarily leaving, 84–87; ways college entrance helped by, 18–25. *See also* admissions, boarding school; daily life, at boarding school; *specific topics*
boarding schools, types of: ultraselective, 169–73
Bolles, 166
Boys' Club of New York, 65
boys' schools: culture and support, 177; military, 178, 187
Brehm, 155, 182
Brewster Academy, 117, 119, 124, 153, 163, 166
Bridgton Academy, 164, 166
Brightbridge Advisors, 14
bullying, 83
Burke Mountain Academy, 125
Buxton, 96

Camden, 178
campus culture, student buy-in of, 21
campus visits, 14–15; cell phones during, 33; common interview questions, 38–41; dress code, 34; interviews during, 31–38, 41–42
Canada, 197
Canterbury, 56, 118, 151, 166
Cardigan Mountain, 178, 179–80, 182; Mountain Day at, 100, 179–80
Caroline D. Bradley Scholarship, 62
Carrabassett Valley Academy, 125, 193
case studies (example scenarios): international students at junior boarding schools, 181–82; involuntarily leaving, 87–89; junior boarding school, 181; learning support success stories, 155–57; postgraduate students (PGs), 159–60, 163–64; student from Kazakhstan, 140–41; students abroad, 195–97; students leaving voluntarily, 84–87
case studies and results: A student with multiple interests, 77–78; athlete/drummer, 79; gifted sophomore, 78–79; lacrosse player/A student, 76–77; theater and music, 77
Cate School, 97–98, 99, 103
cell phones, 33, 95, 96, 186
ceremonies, 99–101
Chatham Hall, 62, 118, 177
cheating, 88
Cheshire Academy, 56, 152, 166
China, 141; applicants from, 142–43; interview service in, 138–39
Choate Rosemary Hall, 35, 56, 111, 121; as choice for dancers, 133; international student percentage, 137; PGs and, 166; prestige and, 170; reclassing and, 180–81; student body diversity, 170; welcome tradition, 94
Christchurch, 118, 123–24
Christ School, 62, 178
Clarity app, 58, 60
coaches: athletic, 32; international students and, 144; recommendations from, 48
college, early, 192
college admissions: acceptance, 9, 17–18, 82–83, 173; boarding school benefits for, 18–25; counselor calls and, 26–28; extracurricular activities and, 22–24; grades importance for, 20–22; prestige factor in, 25–28; recent study on, 19; reclassing and, 10; self-confidence

and, 21; wealth impact and correlation with, 28–30. *See also* ultraselective boarding schools; *specific schools*
communication, 42
community, 4, 93; service, 103–6
competition: between dorms, 98; sports, 101–2, 109; for students in China, 141–42
computer science, 172
concierge services, 144
costs, boarding school, 55, 57, 61; free tuition, 63–64; lowest-priced boarding schools, 56, 63; postgraduate (PG) year, 165; therapeutic boarding school, 158. *See also* financial aid; tuition
counselors and consultants: calls from college, 26–28; college recommendations from, 19–20; educational, 14, 157–58; high school placement advisors, 14; private *vs.* public school, 19–20; recommendations from school, 48, 49. *See also* coaches
Cranbrook, 56, 62, 116, 130–31
critical thinking, 191
Culver Academy, 118, 187, 194; lacrosse teams, 122; scholarships, 62; welcome tradition, 95
Culver Military Academy, 186–87
Curry Ingram, 155
Cushing Academy, 120, 131, 166; learning support success story, 155–56

daily life, at boarding school: ceremonies and traditions, 99–101; community service, 103–6; dining hall and, 98, 102–3; at girls' schools, 176–77; holidays and, 99; jobs and service learning, 103–6; matriculation, 93–95; sports competitions and, 101–2; weekends, 96–98, 100, 101
Dana Hall, 62, 118, 177
dance, 132–33, 176
Darlington, 119, 166
day schools, 88, 137, 142, 190; with homestay, 145–46; lower cost of, 63; scholarships and, 62
dean of admissions, 27, 28
Deerfield, 121, 166, 182; football, 119; formal dinners, 102–3; game day, 101; rowing program, 123; sports competitions, 102; theater program, 134
demographics, 69
dining hall, 98, 102–3
dorms, competition between, 98
dress code, campus visit, 34
Dublin School, 108, 153
dyslexia, 154, 156–57

Eaglebrook, 178, 179, 182; car building elective at, 179; ski area, 124; sports competitions, 102
Eagle Hill, 154, 182
early college, 192
East Coast Prep, 163
educational counseling, 14, 157–58
EF Academy, 62, 197
email, thank-you, 34
Emma Willard, 177
English language, 6, 24–25, 181; tests, 139
enrollment, decision deadline for, 81–82
Episcopal High School, 59–60, *60*, 103, 194; postgraduate students (PGs) and, 116; Spirit Weekend at, 101
equestrian programs, 118
essays, 45–48
Ethel Walker, 118, 177, 182
Eton College, 197

Evert Tennis Academy, 193
exams: neuropsychological, 51, 149–50, 156. *See also* tests and testing
Exeter, 9, 17, 56, 61–62, 101, 123, 166, 172; curriculum, 171–72; football, 119; lacrosse games, 122; Learning Center, 153; music programs and, 132; ultraselective schools and, 170.
expulsion, 83–84, 87–88
extracurricular activities, 22–24

fairs, boarding school, 13
families: access programs for low-income, 65; boarding school list and priorities for, 16; Chinese, 7–8; goals of, 3, 16; late in applying, 11; middle and high-income, 57–58; reclassing decision by, 10
Fay, 182
Fessenden, 178, 182
financial aid, 58–61, *60*; scholarships and, 55
first-choice letters, advocacy calls and, 72–74
Fishburne, 178, 187
football, 101, 108, 118–19, 194
Fork Union, 119, 166, 178, 187
Forman, 154, 166
Fountain Valley, 62, 118
Foxcroft, 118, 177
Frederick Gunn School, 121, 151, 166; applicants from China, 142–43
free boarding schools, 63–64
frequently asked questions, 51–53
friendship, 4, 90

games, 100, 101–2
gaming, 21
gaokao (test for Chinese students), 141

Garrison Forest, 118, 177, 182
Gateway to Prep Schools (application), 44, 46, 47
gender: learning and growth differences based on, 177–78; postgraduate students (PGs) and, 162; single-sex boarding schools, 175–78
George School, 59, 62, 118
Georgetown Prep, 116, 178
Geronimo, sailing cutter, 124
girls: basketball programs for, 118; benefits of all-girls' education, 176; equestrian programs and, 118; hockey programs for, 121; lacrosse, 123; as postgraduate students (PGs) in sports, 116; schools for, 175–77; soccer, 125–26
Glenholme School, 158
golf, 119–20, 193
Gould, 62, 118, 119, 124, 153
Gow, 155
grades, 20–21, 25, 53; inflation, 22, 68
grades (ninth, tenth, etc.): at boarding school entry, 8–9; boarding schools for grades 6 to 12, 182–83; reclassing and, 10
graduation, traditions for, 99
Green Mountain Valley School, 125
Greenwood, 155
Grier School, 62, 118, 132, 153, 177, 182
Groton School, 56, 116, 121, 182; diverse students of, 170; in sports rivalries, 102; Surprise Holiday at, 99
Grove School, 158

Hampshire Country School, 155
Hargrave, 62, 63, 96, 163, 166, 178; as all boys' military school, 187; basketball program, 117; "Eye of

the Tiger" event, 186; phone-free culture of, 186
Headmaster's Holiday, 99
Hebron, 119
Hill, 166
Hillside, 178, 182
historically Black boarding schools, 191–92
Holderness, 105, 124, 166
holidays, 99
home situation, opportunity for improved, 6
homestay programs, day schools and, 145–46
Hoosac, 153
Hotchkiss, 56, 94, 120, 123, 124
Hun School of Princeton, 119, 194

IB. *See* International Baccalaureate diploma
ice hockey, 109–11, 120–22; inquiries about, 112; junior boarding school with, 180
Idyllwild Arts Academy, 135
IECA, 14
IELTS, 139
IEP, 50
IMG Academy, 119, 120, 126, 182, 193; cost and offerings, 56; postgraduate students (PGs) and, 163, 166; sports orientation of, 163; tennis and, 127
Immaculate High School, 146
Independent Educational Consultants Association (IECA), 14
Independent Projects (IPs), 172
Independent School Entrance Exam (ISEE), 50, 51
Independent School League (ISL), 116
Indian Mountain, 183
Indian Springs, 56

individualized education plan (IEP), 50
inquiry form, 43–44
Institute for Educational Advancement, 62
Interlochen Art Academy, 135; Arts Camp at, 135
International Baccalaureate (IB) diploma, 189, 190, 197
International Boys School Coalition, 177–78
International Coalition of Girls' Schools, 176
International English Language Testing System (IELTS), 139
International Junior Golf Academy, 120
international students: admissions committee evaluation and criteria, 142–43; admissions process for, 138–39; boarding school percentage of, 137; Chinese, 141–42; day school with homestay for, 145–46; at junior boarding schools, 181–82; number of, 137; selective schools and admissions, 140–41; tips for thriving at boarding school, 143–45; visas, 137
Internet, researching school websites and, 12–13
Interscholastic Sailing Association (ISSA), 123
interviews: admissions feedback on, 41–42; campus visits and, 31–38, 41–42; common questions during, 38–41; for international students, 138–39; of parents, 36–37; postgraduate students (PG) admissions and, 164; preparing for, 37–38; things to not say or do during, 35–36; third-party service for,

138–39; tips for, 33–34; video conference, 34–35
IPs, 172
ISEE, 50–51
ISL, 116
Island School, 198
ISSA, 123
Ivy League, 17, 109, 110, 163–64; basketball, 117; ice hockey, 121; ultraselective schools and, 169

jobs, service learning and, 103–6
junior boarding schools, 179; international students at, 181–82; list of, 182–83; reclassing at, 180–81
Junior Players Golf Academy, 120

Kent School, 56, 100–101, 118; ice hockey, 121; job programs, 105; rowing program, 108–9, 123; Tapping Ceremony at, 100–101. *See also* South Kent School
Kents Hill School, 119, 124, 151
Killington Mountain School, 125
Kimball Union, 118, 120, 124, 166; learning support program, 152
Knox, 118

lacrosse, 30, 76–77, 122–23
Lake Tahoe Prep, 125
Landmark School, 154
languages, ultraselective school featuring many, 172. *See also* English language
late bloomers, 165
Laurinburg Institute, 191
Lawrence, 116, 153
Lawrenceville, 56, 163, 166; lacrosse history and, 122
LEAD, 151–52
learning differences (learning disabilities), 21; application tests for students with, 50; Eagle Hill reading program and, 154; learning support programs for, 150–53; neuropsychological evaluations and, 149–50; students with, 50, 147–48. *See also* ADHD; learning support
learning support, 51; ADHD and, 86; definition, 149–50; extensive, 151–53; programs, 21, 86, 150–53; schools specializing in, 153–55; soft landing schools and, 157–58; success stories, 155–57
Learning through Enrichment, Analysis, and Development (LEAD), 151–52
Linden Hall, 118, 177
Linsley, 56
loans, 61
Loomis Chaffee, 118, 121, 166

MacDuffie, 182
Madeira, 62, 118, 177
Maplebrook, 155
Marine Military, 178, 187
Marvelwood, 118, 153
Massanutten, 187
Masters School, 97, 131
Master's tournaments, in golf, 120
Mastery School of Hawken, 191
matriculation, 93–95
MaxPreps, 125–26
May Experiential Learning Program, 180
McCallie, 62, 103, 119, 125, 178
Mercersburg, 62, 100, 166; Irving Marshall Week at, 100
merit scholarships, 61–62
Michaels-Dickson Scholars Program, 62
Middlebridge, 155
Middlesex School, 56, 68, 101, 116; acceptances, denials and wait list, 75; admissions committee, 72

military schools, 63, 165; for boys, 178, 187; coed, 187; difference in, 185; list of coed, 187; misconceptions about, 185–86; schools with optional, 187
Millbrook, 105; Trevor Zoo at, 105
Milton Academy, 116, 124, 153; Academic Skills Center at, 153
Miss Hall's School, 25, 118, 177
Missouri Military, 178, 187
Miss Porter's School, 62, 118, 133, 176, 177; "German" welcoming tradition at, 94
Monteverde Academy, 117, 166
move-in day, 93–94
Murex robotics, 171–72
music, 75, 131–32

National Association for College Admissions Counseling, 27
National Association of Therapeutic Schools and Programs, 158
National Basketball Association (NBA), 116, 117, 118
National Football League (NFL), 119, 163
National Hockey League (NHL), 120, 121, 180
National Lacrosse Federation, 122
National Merit Scholars, 12
National Prep Championship, 122
Naval Junior Reserve Officer Training Corps, 187
NBA, 116, 117, 118
need-based financial aid, 57–58
NEPSAC, 117, 120, 121, 124
NESCAC, 121
neuropsychological exams, 51, 149–50, 156
New England Innovation Academy, 190
New England Preparatory School Athletic Council (NEPSAC), 117, 120, 121, 124

New England Small College Athletic Association (NESCAC), 121
New Hampton School, 108, 153, 163, 166
New Mexico Military Institute, 187
New York Military Academy, 187
NFL, 119, 163
NHL, 120, 121, 180
Niche search engine, 13
Nick Bollettieri Academy, 127
Nike Elite Youth Basketball League, 117
NJ Seeds, 65
NMH. *See* Northfield Mount Hermon
nonacademic credentials, 29
nonprofits, access programs of, 65
North Country, 183
Northfield Mount Hermon (NMH), 97, 98, 117, 119, 166; applications from China received by, 142; international admission, 143
Northfield Mt. Vernon, 124
Northwood, 124
notification, decision, 81–82

Oak Hill Academy, basketball program, 117
Oak Ridge, 187
Olympics, 109, 122
Orton-Gillingham approach, 151, 154
Oxford, 155

parents: children of wealthy, 29; college acceptance desire of, 17–18; divorced, 58–59; divorced or separated, 58–59; financial aid questions, 55; house-, 144; international students and, 137–38; interview questions asked by, 40–41; interview questions asked by students or, 40; interviews of,

Index

36–37; separation viewed by, 7–8; student withdrawn by, 84–87; surprising comments of, 89–90
The Parents League of New York, 13
Peddie, 62, 93–94, 120
Pennington, 62, 125
Perkiomen, 62, 182
personal growth, 4, 18–19
PGs. *See* postgraduate students
PG year, 160–64; implications of pursuing, 165; options, 166
Phelps, 178
Phillips Andover. *See* Andover
Phillips Exeter. *See* Exeter
physical education, 108
Pine Forge, 191
Piney Woods, 191–92
plagiarism, 87
policies: alcohol use, 83–84; expulsion, 83–84; one strike, 87; withdrawal and expulsion, 87–88
Pomfret, 62, 166; sample inquiry form, 44
Portsmouth Abbey, 124
postgraduate students (PGs): athletics programs acceptance of, 115–16; case studies, 159–60; gender and, 162; history of PG year, 161–62; number of, 159; reasons for attending fifth year, 9
Prep for Prep, 14, 65
prestige, 25–28, 170
Princeton International School of Math and Science (PRISMS), 190–91
Princeton University, rowing program of, 24
PRISMS. *See* Princeton International School of Math and Science
problems, at boarding schools, 83–84
Proctor Academy, 105, 118, 124, 166; Forestry Research Crew at, 105; welcoming tradition, 94; Woods Team at, 105

PSAT, 50–51
Putney, 118, 166

questions: common interview, 38–41; dance-related, 133; during advocacy calls, 73–74; financial aid, 55; on "first choice," 73–74; frequently asked, 51–53; organizing application form, 46

Rabun Gap-Nacoochee, 62, 119
Randolph Macon, 187
reading programs, 154
reclassing, 10, 108, 165; athletes and, 110; junior boarding schools, 180–81. *See also* postgraduate students
recommendations, 48–49, 68, 71
Rectory, 152, 180
Redemption Christian Academy, 191
relationships, 4
research: creating list of schools as, 15–16; educational consultants and, 14; high school placement advisors, 14; via websites, 12; websites and Internet, 12–13; when to start, 11
Revisit Days, 11, 81, 83, 84
Riverside Prep, 178, 187
Riverview, 155
robotics club, 171–72
Rock Point, 155
Ross School, 56, 62, 182
rowing, 24, 108–9, 123
Rowmark Ski Academy, 125
Rumsey Hall, 181, 183

sailing, 123–24
St. Andrew's School, 100, 103, 153, 194; Arts Weekend at, 100; boarding percentages and, 195; football, 119
St. Catherine's, 178, 183, 187

St. George's, 56, 124; admission committee of, 67–68, 71; number applicants denied, 75; number applicants wait listed and accepted, 75; PGs not allowed by, 116
St. James, 56, 182
St. John's Northwestern, 187
St. Lawrence Seminary High School, 56
St. Margaret's, 177
St. Mark's School, 108, 116
St. Mary's, 177
St. Paul's, 56, 121, 123, 194; dance program, 132
St. Stephen's Episcopal School, 127; theater program, 119, 134, 182
St. Thomas More, 166
St. Timothy's, 118, 177
Salisbury School, 56, 57, 62, 166, 178; ice hockey, 121
San Marcos, 56, 187
Santa Catalina, 177
SAO. *See* Standard Application Online
SAT, 26, 50
schedule, 4, 6
scholarships, 55, 57–58; merit, 61–62. *See also* financial aid
School and Student Services, 58
School for Ethics and Global Leadership, 198
School Profile, 12, 15–16, 83
science, 190–91; computer, 172
screen time, 93, 96, 186
Secondary School Admissions Test (SSAT), 15, 50–51
selective schools, 140–41. *See also* ultraselective boarding schools
semester schools, 197–98
The Semester Schools Network, 197–98
seniors, 9
service learning, jobs and, 103–6

Shattuck St. Mary's, 56, 120, 126, 166, 182; ice hockey, 121–22
Simon's Rock, 192
single-sex boarding schools, 175–78, 187
sit-down dinner, 102–3
skiing, 124–25, 193
soccer, 125–26
social engagement, 93
social media, 4, 21; researching boarding school via, 12
soft landing schools, 157–58
Southern Prep, 178, 187
South Kent School, 68–69, 121, 178
specialty schools: arts and athletic, 193; learning support, 153–55
Spire Academy, 193
sports, 163; at all-girls' schools, 176; athlete levels and, 107; availability of uncommon, 109; competition, 101–2, 109; elite athletes and, 109–11; evaluating athletics programs, 115–16; fall, 125; finding new, 107–9; opportunities for arts and, 5–6; rivalries between schools, 101–2; selected school programs in, 116–27
squash, 126
SSAT. *See* Secondary School Admissions Test
SSV *Tabor Boy*, 124
Standard Application Online (SAO), 44–45, 47, 130
Steamboat Mountain School, 125
STEM, 176, 190
Stevenson School, 56, 120
Stoneleigh Burnham, 118, 177
Stony Brook, 124
Storm King, 182
Stratton Mountain School, 125
Student Health Services, 144
students: accepting postgraduate, 9; age of entry for, 8–9;

boarding school decision made by, 6–7; characteristics sought by admissions committee, 67–69; denied, 75, 78–79; diversity, 170; English language for international, 24–25; essays, 45–46; with good grades, 22; international, 137–46; interview questions asked by, 40; involuntarily leaving school, 87–89; with learning disabilities, 50, 147–48; leaving boarding school voluntarily, 84–87; participation and engagement, 68; questions to ask themselves, 37; readiness in, 6–7; soccer played by new, 125; studying abroad, 195–97; on wait list, 74–76; welcoming traditions for new, 93–95, 99. *See also* postgraduate students; *specific topics*
study time, evening, 95
Subiaco, 178
Suffield, 56, 62, 166
Sugar Bowl Academy, 125
swimming, 126–27

Tabor, 121, 124
Taft, 56, 124, 166
Tallulah Falls, 56
teachers: college recommendations from, 19–20; recommendations from, 48–49, 68, 71
tennis, 127, 193
Ten Schools Admission Organization, 13, 170–71
Test of English as a Foreign Language (TOEFL iBT), 139
tests and testing: English language, 139; *gaokao* for Chinese students, 141; neuropsychological evaluations, 149–50; prep, 51; requirements, 49–50; for students in learning support programs, 51; for students with learning disabilities, 50; types, 50–51
Texas Academy of Mathematics and Science, 192
Thacher School, 118
thank-you email, post-interview, 34
theater, 119, 133–34, 182
therapeutic boarding schools, 157–58
Think Global School, 190
Tilton, 153, 166
TMI Episcopal School, 187
TOEFL iBT, 139
tour guides, 32
traditions: ceremonies and, 99–101; formal dinner, 102–3; girls' school examples of, 176; graduation, 99; student welcoming, 93–95, 99
transcripts, in non-English language, 139
the Traveling School, 198
Trinity Pawling, 21–22, 79, 178, 182; learning support, 151–52; PGs and, 166
tuition: access programs and, 65; annual, 55–57; free, 63–64; loans to cover, 61; merit scholarships for full, 62. *See also* costs, boarding school; financial aid
tutors, 51, 153

ultraselective boarding schools: acceptance rates, 170, 173; defining, 170–71; reputation and desirability, 169–70; students suited to, 173; uniqueness of, 171–72
United World College, 189–90
US Naval Academy, 187
US Senate Page School, 198

Valley Forge, 63, 178, 187
Vanguard, 155
Vericant interview service, 138–39
videos: application including, 46–47; video conference interviews, 34–35

WAIS, 51, 150
wait list, 74–76
Walnut Hill School for the Arts, 135
wealth, college admissions correlation with, 28–30
websites, researching school, 12–13
Wechsler Adult Intelligence Scale (WAIS) tests, 51, 150
Wechsler Intelligence Scale for Children (WISC), 51; WISC-V, 150
weekends, 96–98, 100, 101
Western Reserve, 56, 62, 166
Westminster, 166
Westover, 177
Westtown, PGs not allowed by, 116
Wilbraham and Monson, 166, 182
wilderness orientation, 94
Williston Northampton, 62, 121, 156–57, 166
Winchendon School, 152
WISC. *See* Wechsler Intelligence Scale for Children
Woodberry Forest, 178; Spirit Weekend at, 101
Woodhall, Matt, 154–55
Woodhall School, 154–55

Yale, 30
YouTube, boarding school videos on, 12–13

About the Author

Kristin White is an educational consultant who helps students evaluate boarding schools, colleges, and other educational opportunities while also helping them navigate the admissions process. Kristin's educational consulting firm, Brightbridge Advisors, is based in Darien, Connecticut, but works with students from all over the United States and the world. In the last eighteen years, she has worked with families from nineteen different countries and twenty-two states. Kristin is also the director of high school counseling at a private school in Greenwich, Connecticut, where she helps eighth graders evaluate and apply to high schools.

Kristin is a member of the Independent Educational Consultants Association, where she serves on the schools committee. She is a graduate of Georgetown University and has an MBA from the University of Texas at Austin.

Kristin is the author of *The Complete Guide to the Gap Year: The Best Things to Do between High School and College* and *It's the Student, Not the College: The Secrets of Succeeding at Any College without Going Broke or Crazy*.